Church music
at the crossroads

Seated upon the convex mound
Of one vast kidney, Jonah prays
And sings his canticles and hymns,
Making the hollow vault resound
God's goodness and mysterious ways,
Till the great fish spouts music as he swims.

ALDOUS HUXLEY: Jonah

Where there is no vision, the people perish.

Proverbs 29:18

Church music at the crossroads

A FORWARD LOOKING GUIDE FOR TODAY

Lionel Dakers
Organist of Exeter Cathedral

Foreword by
GERALD H. KNIGHT
Director of the Royal School of Church Music

MARSHALL, MORGAN & SCOTT
London

MARSHALL, MORGAN & SCOTT LTD
BLUNDELL HOUSE
GOODWOOD ROAD
LONDON S.E.14

SBN 551 05246 5

Printed by Willmer Brothers Limited, Birkenhead
and bound by C. Tinling & Co. Ltd., Prescot

Foreword

Never was there a time when the music of our churches relied more upon the amateur organist and choirmaster than today. There is a serious shortage of those who can accompany a service well on the organ, or who can train a choir in such a way that it is efficient and sticks loyally to its twin tasks of leading the singing and saying of the congregation's part and of contributing as well such choral music as is within its competence.

In these conditions, when many an organ stool is occupied by one who might well be described as "a reluctant organist", any help and advice which will add to the self-confidence and increase the effectiveness of such a man or woman, boy or girl, is heartily to be welcomed. There are many therefore, I believe, who will be grateful to Mr. Dakers for this book, into which he has poured much wisdom and common sense based upon contact with things as they are known to him at the present time in the Exeter Diocese, in which he has done and continues to do a fine and self-sacrificing job in trying to help as many as need our help with the music of their churches and who have the necessary graces of humility, patience, and perseverance to make them ready to benefit from it.

It is not, however, just the village organist who can benefit from what is written in this book; the parish priest, the minister, the Reader, and the man in the pew can all learn much that they ought to know and which all too few of them do know about the place of music in worship at a time when the Second Reformation is taking place before our eyes and under our noses. It is hoped that, after reading what Mr. Dakers has said, they will all be able the better to play their parts in the drama of the Church's life today. Here is no voice from the past, no hot air from the cathedral organ loft, no airy-fairy theorising, but rather the down-to-earth and contemporary advice of one who genuinely cares for the Christian cause and sees the part which music could and should play in worship. All who follow his lead will be doing more than improve their music—they will be striking a blow for Christianity itself; for music can make or mar worship; it can bring men to despair by its badness; it can raise them to the throne of God when it is done in the right way and in the right spirit.

GERALD H. KNIGHT

Contents

I Introductory

We live in an age in which our obsession with material things far outweighs our concern for spiritual or eternal values. Because of this the implications of the Christian religion are, for the majority of people, an unattractive and pointless proposition.

The reasons why such a state of affairs exists is not strictly within the province of this book, but the fact that a situation does exist, and a none too healthy one at that, will be apparent from almost every page. There are, however, small but encouraging signs that organised religion in this country is beginning to stage some measure of come-back, bewildered though many people are by the welter of events both spiritual and temporal.

The rethinking of the structure of much of the Liturgy through the processes taking place at the present time, will undoubtedly reshape to a great extent the established pattern of corporate worship. This is a necessary progression which will feed new thought and energy where it is most needed, for certain aspects of the traditions which the Church has accumulated over the centuries and which have produced a formula too static and stereotyped, could to our advantage be dispensed with.

What is exciting and stimulating is the fact that never before have clergy and laity alike been caught up in such widespread and often heated argument on the pros and cons of the reforms now taking place. This in itself is one of the healthiest manifestations we have for the future of the Church, for it shows that many people do in fact care and, moreover, are prepared to take some stand in the matter.

Whatever the future may hold, there is no reason to suggest that voice and instrument will not continue to make a very real contribution to the completeness of our services. For most purposes it matters not how simple or basic that contribution may be; what does matter is that it is done as well as circumstances permit and that it involves everyone—clergy, choir, organist and congregation alike—sometimes separately and sometimes together.

In this book I have tried to show that the witness of the Church can be increased through music well performed. It can just as effectively be retarded by careless and slipshod attitudes for we are *all* capable of much better results than we often realise to be possible.

Much of what I have to say is, on the face of it, depressing. A mere catalogue of niceties might flatter the *ego* of the reader but certainly leave him no better off as a result. That all is not well within the Church is evident to most of us; though whether we are prepared to look critically inwards and see how much of the blame may lie with us is another matter. That all is not well musically is underlined by such factual evidence as the demise, up and down the country, of so many parish church choirs, while those responsible for the music are often, with good reason, discouraged and disheartened.

I shall discuss what seem to me to be the reasons for the conditions which exist in some parishes, though I cannot offer any remedy for the many problems facing us at the present time.

Although my brief was to deal with church music as it affects country areas, I found, as the book began to take shape, that to confine my remarks in this way would have meant omitting reference to many important aspects and side issues. These, as I see it, are the concern of all churches today, no matter where they happen to be situated.

The book is designed to be of help to all organists, especially those who are feeling remote and cut off. I have endeavoured to make organists aware of the responsibilities which are theirs and

I have also made some reference to the Church overseas. This has been included as a result of what I have seen during tours in Africa, India, the Far East and the United States, for there is much we can learn, to our advantage, from the vigour and vitality of the young missionary church in distant lands.

There will inevitably be some repetition and overlapping. This is possibly all to the good and will help to stress certain points of view which I feel are of such importance as to warrant reiteration. I have not hesitated to say what I believe to be true concerning the attitude of some organists—and of some of the clergy. This will no doubt evoke criticism from certain quarters, but one of the objectives of a book such as this must inevitably be to point out what one sees to be faults, as well as virtues, and from them to try to produce something constructive and useful.

The role of the congregation will frequently be stressed. This is an essential part of all corporate worship today: it will be even more so in the new pattern of liturgical worship now emerging. Congregational participation is, in its own right, a highly desirable factor, complementary to the work of the choir; both have their rightful parts to play.

My grateful thanks are due to all who have given me help and advice, whether it has been asked for or not. I am especially indebted to Dr. Gerald Knight, Director of the Royal School of Church Music, for all his comments and suggestions after having read the draft of the book in its final stages. I am also very grateful to Mr. R. S. McDowall, the Editorial Secretary of the Royal School of Church Music. Knowing him to be a human encyclopedia on almost every branch of church music, I automatically turned to him for the information which is contained in the appendices, information which he gave most generously. In doing this he has provided an extremely useful check list for general reference. Mr. Vincent Waterhouse, the Secretary of the R.S.C.M. also gave useful advice concerning Chapter 8. Mr. Alan Gibbs, in Appendix 18, has contributed an informative essay on contemporary trends in the writing of church music. As one of the younger generation of composers now writing for the church he also possesses, as a schoolmaster, practical experience in these and other matters. My thanks are also due to Mr. John Wood who imparted much lively and racy information coined from his own experience.

Finally—and most important of all—to my wife for her help and advice before, during and after I set about my task. So often when I dithered, waffled and fumbled for words she, with an enviable feminine instinct, invariably came up with the right turn of phrase—and at the right moment.

2 Points of departure

1. *The place of music in the worship of the Church today.*

It is doubtful whether the situation today is fundamentally any different from what it ever was. Why do we have music in worship? The Liturgy is complete without it. Nevertheless there is a place for music and it is highly desirable that we should include it in our worship. Vocally, its function is to enrich the meaning of the spoken word: instrumentally, organ music adds to the completeness of a service, providing the music is suitable in mood to the occasion.

Through song there can be a natural expression of joy and emotion. It clothes the words with an added dimension in much the same way that stained glass, vestments and other visual—and colourful—adornments to worship are for many a devotional aid. The reverse can also be true for there are those to whom the trappings of worship are a distraction.

Music in worship should not be a series of disconnected vocal interludes, nor an opportunity merely to stand up and sing because we happen to like singing. Historically, music has always played an integral part in worship, therefore much of the time we spend in church is rightly devoted to it. Judging from some of the results, it is obviously not always appreciated that the ultimate objective which should always be uppermost in the minds of the musicians is that of aiming for as high a standard of performance as is humanly possible. This is a necessity, no matter how simple the music, in the event, may be.

Music is one of the many gifts which God in His goodness bestows on man who, in his turn, uses it to enrich the beauty of worship, be he composer or performer. It is, as Keats saw it, a sense of "beauty in all things", for it is too often forgotten "that beauty is one of the names of God: and to Keats beauty was truth, and truth beauty. He knew this so deeply and intuitively that he felt he needed to know nothing else".[1]

2. *The rôle of the organist and the importance of his task within the Church.*

No matter how simple the music, or primitive the forces at one's disposal, the organist must ensure that his efforts and those of the choir are at all times directed towards the best they can give. This is an objective which demands much of the individual; all of us being human fail in this from time to time, and often without due reason, if we are completely honest with ourselves. Young and old alike, we are far too ready to provide excuses.

Despite the objective of this book as a means of help, it will inevitably by-pass that small but potent group of people who think they have no need of help from anyone. These, alas, are usually the people whose musical house needs more than most to be set in order. Humility and integrity are virtues which have a knack of sometimes evading us.

The organist by his efforts, must inspire choir and congregation alike to sing with understanding. As organist, his main task should always be that of accompanying the singing in such a way that all will compulsively *want* to sing. He must never drive (nor drown) them.

So important is his responsibility in this direction that he can, by his playing, either make or mar any service, as we know only too well. Are organists always aware of the influence they wield?

[1] Contrasts: *The Arts and Religion.* (Alec Robertson). S.C.M. Press, page 15.

3. *Some of the problems facing church music today, especially in country areas.*

The problems which beset many clergy and organists are very real and ever present. This book sets out to suggest how, in some measure, these problems may be overcome. Those who are complacently satisfied with their personal efforts and those of their choir and who see no reason for improvement or change, will obviously find little to their liking in this or any other book on the subject. In an ideal world in which clergy, organists and choirs were all but perfect, there would be no need for books such as this!

As I see it, there are three major aspects which need consideration; these, to a great extent, form the basis of what follows:

(i) Many would produce better results if they knew how to set about it;

(ii) far too many of us have bad habits and do not realise it;

(iii) we need more rehearsal. The lack of this, and of knowing *how* to rehearse, is too readily made the excuse for low standards of performance.

3 The music of the services

Nobody who carries on an ordinary ministry can be unaware of how preposterous and incomprehensible the things he loves most look to anybody in the secular world who notices them at all. No such person interested in church music can ignore the fact that church music seems peculiar, if not downright corrupt, to a secular musician.

Erik Routley: WORDS, MUSIC AND THE CHURCH

THE LITTLE USE WE MAKE OF THE HYMNS AND PSALMS AVAILABLE TO US

Conservatism and a reluctance even to attempt, let alone come to terms with, anything new is at the root of the trouble. Clergy, organists, choirs and congregations are all at some time or another guilty of this. In no other branch of music do sentiment and nostalgia play so prominent or dangerous a part. This sort of bias seems to be one of the occupational pursuits of many who go to church.

We know what we like—even if it is bad. We are quite content with what we know and generally speaking we like it that way. Such is our complacency. Most of us are suspicious and frightened of change but highly pleased with ourselves when we have finally accepted the challenge.

Hymns, though not strictly liturgical, are highly desirable additions to our worship, in fact we could hardly consider our services musical without them. In one form or another they have, from the earliest centuries onwards, played an influential part in Christian worship. St. Augustine, writing in the 7th century, defined a hymn as "a song embodying the praise of God".

How much of the contents of any given hymn book do we use? Of the hymns we sing, how many are repeated frequently, often much more frequently than we realise? In many churches, little attempt is made to widen the choice of hymns. While our inherent conservatism may be partly to blame, we have in the past few years been waking up to the fact that many of our hymns are considerably less valid than we once thought them to be, for they reflect dated sentiments which are irrelevant to the thinking of the Church in the 20th century while others are suspect in their theological content.

If our choice of hymns is narrow and too repetitive we must broaden our outlook and use hymns—both words and music—of many styles and moods, providing the music is a suitable partner for the words. So often, when a Long Metre tune is needed, we plump for a well known tune such as *Wareham,* irrespective of whether its mood suits the words in question. Our defence is that it is "singable". A glance at the index to any hymn book will reveal a surprising number of Long Metre tunes. To instance only one, Sir Percy Buck's *Gonfalon Royal* is music which deserves to be far better known; it is just as singable as *Wareham* and has the added attraction of being more agile and stronger in harmony. This is but one example of many which, with a little thought and care, could be substituted for some of the well-worn favourites. A carefully chosen new tune often gives a revealingly new dimension to a hymn. (See pages 37 and 38).

Choice of hymn book

In all churches such a decision has, at some time, to be taken if only because the existing books are worn out and need replacing.

As far as Anglican collections are concerned, the Standard Edition of *Hymns Ancient and Modern* retains its cosy popularity despite the fact that much of its contents are unsuitable for use today. Its dull format and general look is no recommendation either. The Revised Edition, published in 1950, is a very different proposition and is possibly the best available all-round collection. It contains some fine 20th century words and tunes. But for the fact that many of the tunes, as in the Standard Edition, are pitched too high, it would be an altogether admirable hymn book. Organists are not always acquainted with the fact that a transposed tune book, giving the tunes at a lower pitch, is available from the publishers.

The English Hymnal has very good sections containing a wide choice of Communion and Saints' Day hymns. The influence of Ralph Vaughan Williams, who was the musical editor, is widely in evidence throughout. It is perhaps the most "English" of hymn books and is certainly none the worse for that. It is liberally supplied with Plainsong melodies (is it for this reason that it is sometimes thought of as a "High Church" book?). There are also some very fine early French, German and Italian tunes many of which, considered in their contexts, would have been the "pop" tunes of the time. They are invariably married to some magnificent words from the 6th century onwards, many of them translated by J. M. Neale.

The English Hymnal Service Book, published in 1962, is one of the results of the growth of the Liturgical Movement. While it contains far fewer hymns than its parent book, it makes a point of catering for the needs of the Parish Communion, Mattins and Evensong. All that the average choir and congregation need for any of these services is to be found here including the entire Psalter pointed in speech rhythm, also the responses and Merbecke's setting of the Communion service.

Songs of Praise is not the all-embracing collection it might well have been and it is steadily waning in popularity for a number of very good reasons. The object of the compilers was that it should be a collection of hymns national in character; in the event, it is marred again and again by highly stylised material, much of which is either precious or alien and anyhow fails to ring true. This doctrinaire collection is seen at its worst in the section "For Children" where eccentricity, both in words and music, produces a rarified atmosphere in which nature study, rather than the Christian faith, is pursued with a wholesale relentlessness.

The recent (1967) *Cambridge Hymnal* is in many respects an attempt to come to terms with the need for a realistic collection of hymns for school use. Though it makes no claim to be a hymn book basically geared to the needs of congregational singing as such, it should not because of this be passed by lightly or without careful examination. There is much to be gleaned from it. Leonard Blake, writing in *English Church Music 1968*, (the R.S.C.M.'s annual collection of essays and reviews), said "Everybody concerned with the habitual, institutional use of hymns should study it; and church musicians should be grateful for its provocation, its buoyant break with stuffiness, and its clarion call to truth in our church praise. Whether it will ultimately rank among the hymn books of seminal influence can be left to the judgment of later generations."

One of its most interesting features is the wealth of so much good religious verse, which is more than can be said for the contents of most other hymn books. Even so, it is surprising to see that the Literary Editor, David Holbrook, included only three writers of our own time. All in all however, it is refreshing to find a collection of hymns "unobscured by the dross from the 19th century".

Contemporary trends, including the "pop" element, will be discussed later as will points concerning the performance and "presentation" of hymns. (See Appendix 1 for a recommended list of hymnals.)

PSALMS

> . . . the Psalter, through 90% of its length, has a wisdom, a perceptiveness, and a sense of God's glory which can lift us from where we are *towards* the New Testament as nothing else in literature can.
>
> *Erik Routley:* WORDS, MUSIC AND THE CHURCH

We all too readily sing our hymns, often without giving much thought if any at all, to the meaning of the words, yet we consistently neglect the psalms. It is one of the tragedies of the Church of England today that the average choir and congregation are familiar with only a few of the psalms and usually the shorter ones at that. The words are of such sheer beauty that, quite apart from any other considerations, they contain some of the most beautiful language in our entire Liturgy.

The main deterrents are the practical ones of length and the problems of singing them both effectively and convincingly. Psalmody presents an added difficulty in that no two verses are identical in length or rhythm. Some denominations have partially solved the problem by importing metrical psalms, some of which are of course to be found in Anglican hymn books.

Where the longer psalms are concerned, there is much to commend the singing of certain sections only, provided they are carefully and logically worked out. Nor is there any reason why the psalms should not be said. It is, in fact, much more desirable that they be said well rather than sung badly, the latter being so often in evidence. The slender vocal resources of many country churches—as of some town parishes as well—provide too many obstacles in the way of successfully singing the psalms, though many clergy and organists are of the mistaken opinion that the psalms should, at all costs, be sung, though congregations are seldom provided with that first essential—a pointed psalter.

The singing of the psalms is the most difficult and exacting task which choirs and congregations have to undertake; the pitfalls and snags are legion.

If the psalms are to be said there is little reason for excluding any but it should be emphasised that they must be recited confidently and at a steady pace. The best plan is to say alternate verses antiphonally either between the priest and the congregation or, better still, antiphonally between the two sides of the church. Anglican congregations in this country can rarely be cited as shining examples of how best to deal with the spoken parts of the services, and by no means all of the clergy are models. Congregational mumbling, often at an incoherently gabbled pace, is a habit much in evidence; it does little to enhance worship but much to effectively destroy the beauty of the language we are privileged to have inherited.

Where the singing of the psalms is concerned, *The Parish Psalter* is, for most practical purposes, by far the best. It is basically simple in its pointing and easy to read; it also promotes the best aspects of speech rhythm. *The Oxford Psalter* and *The*

Worcester Psalter are workable examples of speech rhythm pointing, especially the latter, but the visual aspect of the printed page is in both instances formidable and more complicated to follow.

The Cathedral Psalter and *The New Cathedral Psalter*, (respectively black and red), are still popular in many churches despite the clumsy and often un-natural methods which they employ in the pointing. As with *The Parish Psalter*, both are provided with chants, some of which are more readily acceptable than others.

In the final count, any psalm singing, be it from the blackest of Cathedral Psalters or from the latest in speech rhythm, will make good sense only when sung lightly and—above all else—intelligently.

Two recent publications worthy of consideration are *The Revised Psalter* and the psalmody of Joseph Gelineau. The former is the work of the Archbishops' Commission to revise the Psalter, comprising a distinguished group of theologians, musicians and poets including T. S. Eliot and C. S. Lewis. Their task was to revise the text of the existing Psalter so as to remove "obscurities and serious errors of translation, yet such as to retain, as far as possible, the general character in style and rhythm of Coverdale's version and its suitability for congregational use". The result is a smoothly flowing text admirably and simply pointed on the lines of *The Parish Psalter*.

While in itself there is in every respect much to commend this new version, it has already come up against some opposition mainly from those who, as a matter of principle, resent *any* change within the Church or from those who for reasons best known to themselves, cannot (or will not) come to terms with any alteration to the familiar pattern of words they have known all their lives, even though the old version is often very obscure or even inaccurate.

The psalms as dealt with by Father Gélineau, a French priest musician, are more easily accepted, possibly because the style of approach and treatment is quite different from the familiar Anglican style of pointing. Some people seem more readily able to come to terms with a complete breakaway rather than a version, such as *The Revised Psalter,* in which side by side with much that is familiar are new versions which serve as irritants.

The Gélineau psalms can be performed in a variety of ways and the repeated use of an antiphon, or refrain, can be sung by the congregation while the choir or even a solo voice can sing the psalm verses as they occur. The "new look" in the language, together with the attractively simple melodic outlines employed, have combined to make a considerable impact and a degree of popularity which is being generally maintained. (See pages 132 and 133).

Whatever the shortcomings—and there must inevitably be some—of the *The Revised Psalter* as with the Gélineau psalms, they do at least represent some measure of a contemporary attempt at coming to terms with the recurring problems of singing the psalms in a satisfying manner. Experimentation as such, though it has not until recently been a prominent aspect of Anglican worship, is a necessary part of the work of the Church and something which is now being accepted as inevitable. (See Appendix 2 for a list of published Psalters).

CHANTS

While there is always much discussion—often heated—on "good" and "bad" hymn tunes, organists and clergy are by contrast often curiously uninterested where the choice of chants is concerned. While there are some very beautiful chants to draw on, a considerable number are either nondescript or merely dull. This so often applies to single chants, many of which tend to sound more or less alike. In this context, it is difficult to be adventurous, let alone inspired, within a melodic framework of ten notes. Few single chants can be classed as masterpieces of harmonic or melodic invention.

Experience shows that some chants sing better than others and it is helpful to remember certain pointers. Avoid chants in which the reciting note is high or contains discordant harmony; care will need to be exercised in matters of balance:

Here the tenors and basses singing the high D will have to restrain themselves from the understandable temptation of producing too much sound, otherwise they will obscure the comparatively low melodic line. It is best to avoid, whenever possible, dotted notes and passing notes; they tend to sound fussy and they hold up the natural flow of the words—a consideration which must be at the root of all good pointing. For these reasons they are difficult to negotiate well and are in many instances best omitted:

is much smoother and easier to sing when altered to:

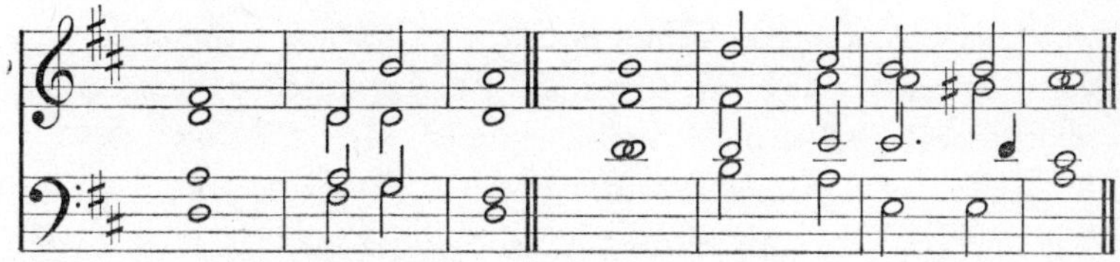

A glance at the chants in *The Parish Psalter* will illustrate the practical application of this principle.

Changes of chant, when used within a psalm, must be reasonably smooth. The new chant must be chosen with care so that the change does not jar either vocally or harmonically.

Remember that whereas by nature most hymns are essentially congregational, psalms are not. Because of this, choir and organist alike must give a firm lead otherwise the congregation will either give up under the difficulties, or, in battling on against all odds, contribute further chaos.

Appendix 3 lists various collections of chants. In addition to this, some churches—and most cathedrals—have their own private, and generally unpublished, collections. *The Anglican Chant Book,* recently published by Novello, is worth careful inspection. In order to compile it, almost every chant book in existence was examined. Dr. Gerald H. Knight, Director of the Royal School of Church Music, has referred to the result as "easily the most comprehensive of all chant books".

OTHER MUSICAL ASPECTS OF THE SERVICES WITH SOME THOUGHTS ON PERFORMANCE

The Parish Communion

This must claim our attention first since it is rapidly assuming, in so many parishes, the prominence which rightly attaches to it. This makes it, as a central act of corporate worship, the most important service there is even to the extent of usurping Mattins in parishes where Mattins has held pride of place for many years. In referring to this, Canon Waddams of Canterbury Cathedral says "the Holy Communion service is an act of the whole People of God, of the congregation of the faithful coming together to do something in common. Their musical part should therefore express this basic truth for, if it does not, the whole service will be greatly weakened in its Christian impact, both for them and for the visitor who comes in from outside. In practice this means that the fixed parts of the service should be mainly, and usually totally, congregational in character." He goes on to say "How much of the fixed text should the people sing if we adopt the liturgical principles already mentioned? They should certainly sing the Creed, the Gloria, the Sursum Corda and Sanctus, and the Our Father. It cannot be too strongly stressed that the *common* singing (or saying) of the Our Father is the climax of prayer of the Holy Communion service and everything should be done to encourage maximum participation by the people, for it is the prayer in which we approach God in unity with

Christ whose prayer it is." (The Music of "Series II". The Holy Communion Sung. (Church Music Society Occasional Paper No. 25.)

The time at which the Parish Communion takes place also favours its popularity as it leaves the rest of the day free. A service commencing at 11 a.m. is less likely to become a family service than one at 9.30 a.m. This, plus the fact that most wives have a Sunday lunch to cook, reflects in some degree the changes in our way of life compared with 20 or 30 years ago.

More important still is the fact that the drama, and therefore the action, of the Eucharist has much more appeal to all age groups than have other services. It is this "action" of the Eucharist (action is the all-important dividing line between the Eucharist and the static nature of the Offices) which demands "togetherness" by *all* involved, be they priest, servers, choir or congregation. All have an important part to play in the moulding of the whole.

The experimental Series Two service, with so much more for the congregation to do, pushes one stage further the processes of corporate worship which have been developing so noticeably during recent years. This is to be seen also in breaks with tradition such as a layman (or laywoman) reading the Epistle and in the Offertory Procession.

The music of the Eucharist has always presented problems, especially when congregational involvement is concerned. For a number of good reasons, Merbecke still retains pride of place as *the* one essentially congregational setting—a strange fate when one remembers that it was never written with that purpose in mind. Martin Shaw's *Folk Mass,* written 400 years later, but in an idiom not without its similarity, comes one stage further but is not the musical ideal. What is lacking in Merbecke's treatment of the words is seen at its worst in *Gloria in excelsis*; here, the lugubriously low melodic line is coupled to an almost complete lack of imagination in relation to the magnificence of the words. It is strange that even in some of the best settings of the Mass the *Gloria* is so often the weakest part. It must be said that in most other respects, despite its severe austerity, the vocal range of Merbecke, together with the fact that it is well known, makes it readily commendable to the majority of parishes. Its presentation generally needs to be much more imaginative than is suggested by the heavily plodding way in which it is so often sung. Phrases sung by men's voices contrasting with sopranos make for the same sort of interest as by singing some phrases unaccompanied. These are variants which help to increase the all round potential of the music.

The length and nature of the *Creed*—which ideally ought to be sung, or said, by *all*—presents many problems. Apart from the extended settings of composers of the stature of Stanford (which are anyhow in a class of their own and not intended for congregational use), Kenneth Leighton, in the *Creed* of his Communion Service in D has, in a bold march-like unison, probably come nearer to the answer than anyone else. He has contrived to combine an innate sense of the meaning of the words with a compelling melodic line which is not unduly difficult to sing. It is unfortunate that the remainder of this service is so technically demanding, or even impossible, for the average organist to cope with even though the voice parts are less exacting. The music was constructed so that it could be sung in three different ways—one of them congregation alone—and all equally effective.

Another practical problem is the reluctance on the part of many congregations, no matter how simple the music, to sing out boldly and with conviction. A similar attitude towards the said parts of the services will be mentioned later.

Even if a really conclusive 20th century successor to Merbecke has yet to emerge, much experimentation is happily taking place. Bryan Kelly's recent (1968) communion service is a follow-up to his highly successful *Magnificat* and *Nunc Dimittis* based on Latin-American rumba rhythms. The Congolese *Missa Luba,* although hardly suitable for general use, does at least point the way in rhythmic content, an aspect of choir and congregational singing which need to be constantly in mind if vitality and drive is to be an obvious part of our services. In this respect the world of secular music provides plenty of competition, some of it highly exciting.

In the end, if it means reverting to Merbecke, the triumphant parts of the service such as the Creed and to a certain extent the *Gloria in Excelsis* must be sung and played with a maximum of authority. In the Creed the organist needs to give a really compelling lead in what is, after all, the affirmation of our belief and of what religion is concerned with. Such an approach will help to make everyone think again—an important process, for much of our organised religion tends through its repetitiveness to lead to parrot-fashion recitation.

A list of settings of the Communion service, together with some indication of the degree of difficulty involved, is given in Appendix 4.

A number of churches have introduced so called "popular" settings emanating from the 20th Century Church Light Music Group. Music such as Patrick Appleford's *Mass of Five Melodies* and the compositions of the controversial Beaumont leave much to be desired both musically and in general taste. Although these composers have a certain following, the style in which they write is far from being truly contemporary, savouring as it does of the light music idiom of the 1930's plus an overdose of cloying sentiment. Sincere as these compositions may be, one cannot in all honesty see in them a degree of permanence which will cause them to become seriously integrated into the Liturgy. The workmanship and inspiration is questionable and the mood so self-consciously alien. Is this perhaps partly due to the fact that, unlike Leighton, Kelly—or even Merbecke—these composers are amateurs?

Whatever the shortcomings of their music may be, we must credit these composers with making some attempt at coming to terms with the popular needs of today. Even if their own compositions may be shortlived they have done useful pioneer work towards what may well be a new dimension of religious expression.

In the Parish Communion more than in any other service there is need to give much thought to the choosing of hymns, bearing in mind always their relevance to particular places in the service. For example, the hymn at the Offertory must be long enough for all that has to be done at the Altar at that juncture. Similarly, the final hymn after the blessing should either be one of thanksgiving or relevant to the particular season or occasion. If the church has no choir, the choice of hymns must be made with even more care. Many hymns are, for various reasons, less suitable than others for congregational use. Each hymn has in the end to be judged on its own merits and suitability.

Mattins and Evensong

> ... It is now widely held that morning and evening prayer are an unsatisfactory compromise—too rigid, too unadaptable to the condition of people who come only occasionally, too firmly dependent on the historical fact that they are meant to be daily, not weekly, services. A weekly service for a scattered congregation is disproportionately short if it lasts only twenty minutes; so morning and evening prayer are lengthened by various additions, notably by the addition of a sermon and of extra prayers and congregational hymns. These additions are not provided for in the injunctions which prescribe the order of these services.
>
> *Erik Routley:* WORDS, MUSIC AND THE CHURCH

Of the two, Mattins tends to be far less attractive than Evensong. This is possibly because of the length of the canticles at Mattins and of the time of day when it usually takes place. The monastic origins of the Offices prevent them from becoming readily congregational; whatever degree of participation may be achieved is done by means of intrusion rather than by integration. This is surely one of the reasons why Mattins in particular, with its long canticles or psalmody, seems uneventful and meandering. By contrast, the very nature of the Eucharist with its action and its togetherness does exactly the opposite.

There is much to be said for commencing at "O Lord, open thou our lips"; this was the original start to the service and by doing so we avoid the "wordy" penitential section provided by the 1662 Book of Common Prayer. In any case, it is questionable whether Mattins and Evensong are the correct places for the use of confession.

Musical settings of the canticles at either service are out of context and entirely unsuitable in all but a relatively few parish churches where the musical tradition warrants this and where the musical resources are considerable.

The provision, in the original version of Series Two Mattins, for using only one of the three traditional sections of *Te Deum* at any given time would seem to be a highly sensible procedure with much to commend it. It would help to cut down the long bouts of psalmody.

It cannot be emphasised too often that the satisfactory singing of the psalms will only be achieved through constant care and practice.

Anthems

For the average country church with small musical resources, anthems, if they are to be performed at all, need to be simple. Appendix 5 lists a wide variety of easy but interesting anthems, none of them making unreasonable demands on either choir or organist.

Mention will be made later concerning the value of introducing new hymns as choir anthems. This supplies a two-fold function for as well as presenting a new tune to the congregation it provides a platform for the choir. There is also much to be said for using psalms as anthems. Of this, Dr Routley has said "they speak of human experience, and often of personal experience, and they are part of the sacred literature upon which the Christian faith rests; more particularly, they are part of the sacred literature in which our Lord himself was brought up".

Whatever a choir attempts in the way of an anthem must of necessity be well performed. This aiming for—and maintaining—a standard cannot be stressed too much or too often. The anthem is the one place in the service where the choir ought to excel in its own right and it must always be remembered that the congregation have perforce to listen to the efforts of the choir. If a choir produces good results it will have provided an aid to worship; if otherwise, nothing more than an unpleasant distraction which can easily become an embarrassment to all.

The congregation will listen the more attentively if they are told the words of the anthem or, better still, have the words in front of them. Some of the best choirs in the land are guilty of shoddy articulation.

The singing of an anthem to help pin-point festivals or other special occasions can be a useful aid in helping to promote one aspect of evangelism.

Versicles and Responses

The tradition, which still lingers on in some parishes, of singing elaborate responses is on all counts to be discouraged. Versions such as the so-called "Tallis Festal" are, as usually encountered, of doubtful authenticity. They are thickly harmonised and the fact that choirs often sing the time values exactly as written obviates any degree of the rhythmic freedom in interpretation which ought to be the basis of successfully singing any responses. The factor which finally outrules such settings is that they are out of step with the simplicity which should be the aim when singing responses in parish churches.

For practical purposes, the neatly printed R.S.C.M. Ferial Responses cannot be bettered. They can be sung either as SATB (with or without organ) or by unison voices with organ accompaniment. The Lesser Litany can be either said or sung. For most occasions the former is best as it enables the Creed and Lord's Prayer to be said by all in a natural voice. Even in most cathedrals nowadays the Creed is said. This procedure, as far as parish churches are concerned, dispenses with the necessity, in most instances, of having to accompany the Creed in order to maintain the pitch. Most of the harmonised versions of the Creed are unbelievably bad, overloaded as they are with an excess of sugary and sentimental harmony of the worst type. Intoning —and staying on the note—is one of the hardest of disciplines which singers have to contend with and many first rate choirs run into difficulties here from time to time. A vicar who cannot intone properly becomes, in the eyes of the choir, something of a marked man. Frustrating though some of us may find this to be, it must always be remembered that singing is for the majority of clergy very much of a sideline and something which is often embarrassing for them to have to do in public Even so, the incidence of tone deafness among the clergy must surely be higher than in any other branch of the populace.

As in successful psalm singing, so in responses the essence of success is speech rhythm. Responses are made the more difficult by being essentially miniatures, many of which end almost before they have begun. Long or short, they need to be sung lightly and with due care for the tidiness of the final consonants. Avoid the lethargic "s" of "us" which causes the word in so many instances to sizzle or sound like "uzs". Final words such as "salvation" and "joyful" can, and do, so often become distorted into "salva-SHERN" and "joy-FULL" instead of "sal-*VA*-tion" and "*JOY*-ful"—in other words, the "shading off" of the final syllable is essential.

Singing the final response "And take not thy Holy Spirit from us" both slowly and softly, is a strange tradition. If we ask the Almighty for the Holy Spirit to remain with us, surely our response ought to be a fervent one?

Said parts

It is highly desirable, for obvious reasons, that everyone take part in such sections of the services as are directed to be said by all. It is, moreover, the duty of everyone to do so as part of a community which has come together to worship together. A clear and definite lead must be given by the choir as a firm basis for the congregation.

It is unfortunate—to say the least—that clergy, choir and congregation so frequently combine to mumble their way through these parts of the service in such a manner as to give the impression that they are either bored or uninterested. This adopting of an unnatural "ecclesiastical" voice once one is at service is one of the most indefensible and stupid things connected with churchgoing.

The parsonic voice is by no means a thing of the past. In churches where it lingers on, the faithful parishioner learns to live with the weekly sound of his vicar's voice. After a while it isn't funny any more and the chances are that, despite his voice, he is a first-rate parish priest who talks quite naturally anywhere but in church. This is the sort of thing which makes it all the more ponderous. For the casual or non-churchgoer seeing the television programme "Gas and Gaiters", it is something of a revelation (if and when he does go to church) to find that the vicar does perhaps talk like Derek Nimmo.

Anglican worshippers in this country are notoriously slack over the said parts of the services. We can learn much from our Free Church brethren and from the Anglican Church overseas where many parishes go about such things in a more convincing and often inspiring way. They are not afraid to proclaim what they believe and they say it boldly without the seeming necessity of burying their heads in their hands during the process. This applies also to Amens, which can so often deteriorate into a grumbling noise which sounds like "*Ar*men".

If the choir is not taught to give a good lead in these matters or, worse still, if choirmaster and choir alike cannot be bothered to spend time over a few non-musical—but important—things, they should rethink their ideas. Everything a choir does, from singing Amens to processing, is of the utmost importance in the correct ordering of worship. It must also always be remembered that the majority of choirs sit in a position where they are visible to most of the congregation.

Music at Weddings and Funerals

The choice of music at these services is sometimes deplorable. While the wishes of those about to be married must obviously be considered, as must the wishes of the relatives of a deceased person, the music which they suggest is, in many cases, chosen merely for sentimental reasons.

The Church, as an institution, is frequently used by non-churchgoers as a convenient place for a wedding; it is more "proper" (whatever that means) than a Registry Office. This making use of the Church leads, in many instances, to a choice of music quite unsuitable to the service in question. While trying to meet the wishes of those most closely concerned, the clergy, who are ultimately responsible for permitting the music, should make it quite clear from the start that the Book of Common Prayer provides a service for the occasion and that the music must at least have something in common with this. Unfortunately, the ways of putting this into practice vary greatly from one parish to another. The addition of a conglomeration of musical extras should be discouraged.

In weddings, is the fact that the Duchess of Kent walked down the nave to the Toccata from Widor's Fifth Symphony sufficient excuse in itself for Miss X and a thousand other brides to follow suit?

There are many suitable alternatives to Mendelssohn's *Wedding March*. Five reasonably easy examples taken more or less at random, are.

Purcell: Trumpet Voluntary.
Purcell: Trumpet Tune and Air.
Handel: March from *The Occasional Oratorio.*
Handel: Allegro (in D major) from *The Water Music.*
Mozart: Wedding March from *The Marriage of Figaro.*

The Prayer Books of 1662 and 1928 provide a surprisingly wide choice of psalms. There is no justification for substituting a metrical version, such as Psalm 23 to *Crimond*—a psalm which, as it happens, is not included in the Marriage Service.

At funerals one can only plead for the inclusion of words and music which reflect some measure of thanksgiving for the life of the departed one. The singing of someone's favourite hymn is one thing but music indicative of a morbid outlook on death is a very different and less desirable proposition. The choice of music for a funeral sometimes reflects an almost hysterical preoccupation with grief—and with it a morbid undercurrent of finality—rather than a concern for the Christian hope and belief in a future life.

4 Good music versus bad music —and why

We so often hear the remarks "only the best will do". This is a statement which, as far as church music is concerned, covers a multitude of sins, most of them of error or omission.

How can we define, in so many words, what particular qualities define "the best"? Music which is satisfactory to one person may well produce a completely opposite reaction from another, yet both will put up a reasoned opinion and sometimes even a convincing case. Personal taste, background and environment are all, in some degree or other, deciding factors. For many of us, left to our own devices and with perhaps only a limited experience in these matters, some guidance and help is both a comfort and a yardstick.

A country organist, paddling his own canoe, will often—with every reason—feel cut off or isolated. He must take every opportunity to seek the advice of someone who really knows and can guide him in deciding what music should, or should not, be included in the services. More of how to go about this in a moment.

One thing is certain without asking anyone's advice: never be misled by the apparently popular appeal of any one piece of music. Popularity does not necessarily imply that music is good. With this in mind, organists must resist, as far as they can, the all-too-familiar parish pattern of events whereby one is asked (or told) to perform music either because the vicar's wife likes it or because the local squire (who perhaps helps to keep the church solvent) is devoted to a certain hymn tune. Instances such as this—and they do occur—need to be handled with great tact especially as the organist is not usually in a very good bargaining position. Sometimes, in fact, the pistol is at his head.

Whatever the situation, one or two pointers may be of help to organists:

1. Your cathedral organist ought to be the obvious person to whom you feel you can go for advice. If however you know he is the type of cathedral organist who cannot be bothered with the problems of a country organist (and there are still a few whose minds work in that way) save yourself the bother of getting in touch with him; anyhow, he possibly won't answer your letter, stamped addressed envelope or not. Similarly, the organist of the major parish church in the area ought to be able to give some help in the matter but do not necessarily rely on him; strangely inadequate organists are to be found enthroned in some of our more important parish churches.

The most reliable course is to seek the advice of the Royal School of Church Music. Their graded lists of church music have been compiled over the years by experts and are for many of us a valuable mine of information concerning every category of church music. Acting as an information bureau is but one of the many functions of the R.S.C.M. in the cause of raising the standards of church music.

2. Every generation has produced good, bad and indifferent music, therefore avoid generalisations. To assume that *all* Victorian music must of necessity be bad and *all* contemporary music good is to be seriously misled. Knowing what to avoid is what matters most.

3. Standards of performance enter very much into an assessment of music. The style of any one particular piece of music can easily be misrepresented in its interpretation because what sounds pleasing when sung by one choir can sound most unattractive when sung by another. Performances on radio or gramo-

phone records by reputable choirs and organists are a generally safe yardstick for judging the merits of the music.

4. Never shun music which is simple. The fact that it is simple and straightforward may well be one of the virtues to commend it. In this respect a choirmaster ought, on all occasions, to cut his coat according to the cloth.

Generally speaking, elaborate music—if it is to be performed with any degree of standard—demands a degree of technique and musicianship far in advance of the resources of the average parish church. Organists ought to have this constantly in mind, for relatively simple music well sung is more rewarding to listen to than an indifferent performance of difficult music.

5. Much church music, especially hymns, is in fact *bad* Victoriana. Some fearsome examples of the worst types of Victorian music are still perpetrated, in some cases by choirs whose organists ought to have better taste. The worst examples are symptomatic of the cloying sentimentalism which was one of the less enviable features of the era. Much Victorian church music was written by amateurs who thought in terms of the organ rather than voices; this resulted in an excess of slow moving chordal music most of which lacked any influence coined from the best vocal traditions of previous generations.

6. At the present time much is being said and written about the validity of many of our hymns. This in itself is good and shows that we have at last realised that many of the hymns which bring back childhood memories and associations are not as good as we once thought they were. Hymns today—and the way in which we sing them—must be relevant to the drastically altered day and age in which we find ourselves.

Canon Adam Fox, himself by no means a young person, was enlightened enough to recently write "Many hymns must be swept away, however much favoured, because they do not reflect the mind of the age, or more precisely because they don't use the images which are in the modern mind of the socially conscious, science conditioned, world ranging, adult man of today".

That we must widen our vision concerning hymns is certain

but it is equally certain that the answer does not lie in the "pop" element. To quote Dr. Routley yet again, "Most pop tunes are in themselves so uninteresting as to offer no competition even to second-rate church music, and there is simply nothing to be gained by importing them into the church as tunes".

Some of the more positive elements which may help us to assess good qualities in music and its performance are:

(a) Melody, harmony and rhythm must go hand in glove in partnership, each complementing the other. The lack of rhythmic sense is one of the worst features of hymn singing today, while phrasing and punctuation are often little better.

(b) Choral music *must* reflect the spirit of the words and, in some positive way, enhance their meaning. We sometimes fail so miserably in this respect. Sir Edward Bairstow once wrote that "song is speech beautified". His anthem *Though I speak with the tongues of men* is an inspired example of this with magnificent words not only superbly set but enhanced by the music.

In our pursuit of music we all too often forget that, as far as choral music is concerned, the words are the point of departure and the music complementary to them.

The following are some examples of hymns where the intermarrying of words and music is most successful:

(i) Vaughan Williams' tune *Sine nomine* admirably partners the strength of Bishop Walsham How's fine words. "For all the Saints".

(ii) The use of *Hyfrydol* to "Love Divine, all loves excelling" gives an added breadth and spaciousness to the words. Stainer's uneventful tune, which is usually associated with Charles Wesley's magnificent words, has a completely opposite effect and, by contrast, contrives to make the words sound insignificant. Boyce's *Halton Holgate,* (*A and M* 186), is a much happier choice for these words. It is in every way a fine tune and it goes just as effectively to Newman's "Firmly I believe and truly".

(iii) Somervell's tune to "Praise to the holiest" (*A and M Revised* 185) originally written for his *Passion of Christ* (a very worthy little work in its own right). It makes a good second alternative to the more familiar *Richmond* and *Gerontius*.

(iv) "Lead, kindly light" to *Alberta* by Sir William Harris. The central theme of the words is movement yet Dykes's tune is for ever stopping and starting. Harris's tune has a much more compulsive rhythm and the sense of direction is never in question.

(v) Nicholson's *Bow Brickhill* is one of the best tunes of its time. The broad spaciousness of its melodic line is allied to a strong harmonic sense, especially in the second half. In the 1950 edition of *A and M* it is set to the words "We sing the praise of him who died", with the austere *Breslau,* which does little to enhance these fine words, relegated as an alternative tune.

(vi) The fine tunes of Orlando Gibbons as found in *The English Hymnal.* All, without exception, not only seem to partner the words to an admirable extent but even add to their stature. In particular, 98, 259, 384 and 413 are specially to be commended.

(vii) Finally, when a Common Metre tune is needed, take a look at *Credition* (E.H. 206). It is a simple but shapely melody with good supporting harmony. It goes especially well to "The Church of God a kingdom is".

In the final count, be it hymns, anthems or settings, it is always a matter for deciding—and this is never all that easy—what is liturgically suitable. The music—and the words—must not only stand up to the test of inevitably frequent repetition but, for both performer and listener, they ought to produce a new and inspiring experience each time they are sung. How often does this happen?

Appendix 6 lists R.S.C.M. publications which may be helpful in choosing music.

5 The congregation

THEIR ACTIVE ROLE

The part played by the congregation is best seen as being complementary to the function of the choir. The clerical line of thought which argues that while we have choirs, congregations will continue to sing in a half-hearted manner or not at all, is merely an assumption. There is no guarantee whatever that the disbanding of choirs would improve congregational singing; the very opposite effect is more likely to result in most parishes.

As we have already seen, liturgical trends provide an opportunity today for a much greater degree of congregational participation than ever before. This is part of a continuing process which has been gaining in momentum ever since the publication in 1922 of the report "Music in Worship". These trends are not confined merely to singing. Not everyone is capable of singing (or wishes to sing), nor will every member of the congregation necessarily find himself reading the Epistle or taking part in the Offertory procession, but everyone can—and should—take an active part in those sections of the service which are intended to be *said* by all.

This applies so forcibly in the Parish Communion and to such an extent, if Series Two is used, that one of the prime objectives of this experimental service is defeated if the congregation remain passive and silent.

If then, an active role is to be taken by the members of the congregation and is to make any measurable contribution to the worship of the Church, it must be done well. To take but one example, the *Sursum Corda,* sung to the traditional Sarum Tone, can be very impressive if sung well. It can be even more dramatic in its impact when an entire congregation, in *saying* it, almost thunders out the responses "We lift them up unto the Lord". I have heard this in Singapore Cathedral and I shall long remember it, but it was memorable only because of the compulsive way in which the Dean said "Lift up your hearts".

If then, for the future, the stress is rightly to be centred to a much greater extent than before on congregational participation, the resulting sounds must be the best of which we are capable and to this end the congregation must be prepared to practise its part, in much the same way as choir, servers and even bell-ringers all rehearse their respective roles.

There is little reason to doubt that hymn singing will continue to retain its popular place as the staple diet of most church music. If it is going to be an attractive proposition to young and old alike, it must be earmarked by a compelling rhythmic drive, together with a very real awareness of the words and their meaning. The continuation in many parishes of the age-old dreariness of much of our organised worship, together with the slapdash way in which it is presented, is a very real and continuing deterrent to would be churchgoers, especially of the younger generation. Congregations have, in no uncertain way, a missionary role to play and they can do much to present the Church as a virile and up-to-date organisation, but only if they themselves think that way and act with confidence and conviction.

While present trends exist in the structure of society (and there would seem to be little hope of an appreciable change in the forseeable future), we shall continue to see the slow decline of choirs in many parishes. Sad though this is, it is nevertheless an inescapable fact of today and it places a greater burden than ever upon the congregation.

Most choirs and organists are keen to learn new music. A few, who cannot be bothered to do so, plod on in the well worn paths with an attitude of mind which is sometimes evidenced by their performance. With congregations it is a very different matter. The built-in conservatism of the average congregation can be a very formidable obstacle when it comes to introducing anything new and unfamiliar, yet most of the people who automatically resent *anything* new in the content of the services are seldom able, when cornered, to put forward any really convincing reasons for their objections.

Nevertheless, conservatism for its own comfortable sake can sometimes, as far as music is concerned, be surmounted—if one goes about it in the right way.

The fiercest battles are likely to be fought over hymns. In the end it is all a matter of elementary psychology, for the root of the problem is usually resentment by a congregation at having something unexpectedly new thrust upon them. Nothing upsets more than the unheralded appearance of a new tune in place of one of the old favourites. Resentment under such circumstances is justified. A new tune introduced two or three weeks in advance as an anthem by the choir, or played as an organ voluntary if there is no choir, will cause far less trouble than by springing it on the congregation without warning. A word or two of explanation by the vicar as to why it is being introduced will also help to sugar the pill.

All this will not of necessity ensure that the congregation will take to the new music at once—or at all—but it will at least have shown the congregation that they have been taken into the confidence of the vicar and the organist. An important part of the process is to repeat the new tune at frequent intervals.

Even so, there are likely to be inevitable repercussions especially from the diehards. Whatever changes are contemplated or made in the Church, especially when they cut across firmly established traditions, can always be guaranteed to upset some people but the vitality of the Church is the more important long term consideration. Innovations and a new look there must be if the future health and vigour of the Church is to be assured.

As was mentioned earlier, hymns must be carefully chosen. In most parishes it is generally unwise to attempt to replace well established favourites—as far as the music is concerned—unless there is very strong justification for such action. A personal preference on the part of the vicar or the organist is not always a sufficient reason in itself. Substituting Sir William Harris's *Alberta* for the dreary Dykes' tune to "Lead, kindly Light" is one matter; to attempt to introduce a new tune to "Abide with me" is to ask for trouble in no small measure as well as being one of the surest ways of putting the proverbial cat amongst the proverbial pigeons. Despite this, those who object to change need to be reminded that the old favourites were once new, even though it may have been many years ago.

Despite the criticisms which will accompany changes, go your way with a convinced and undeterred confidence—if you really are convinced of the validity of what you are doing. Always bear in mind local conditions, together with the personnel and ability of your choir.

Whatever you do, take comfort from the fact that you will never please everybody!

6 Training the choir—its many aspects

"It's always best on these occasions to do what the mob do."
"But suppose there are two mobs?" suggested Mr. Snodgrass.
"Shout with the largest," replied Mr. Pickwick.

Charles Dickens: PICKWICK PAPERS

Are Choirs necessary? Very definitely yes, provided that they sing and behave well.

A good choir can be of great assistance not only by singing music which is beyond the capacity of the congregation, but also by its demeanour and deportment it can add to the dignity of the service. It can also inspire the congregation to take an active part in the singing.

The existence of a good choir provides the Incumbent with a nucleus of faithful people who can assist him by word and example in the spiritual life of the parish.

Gerald H. Knight: TWENTY QUESTIONS ON CHURCH MUSIC

Much of the work involving the choir has been discussed elsewhere in this book. As many excellent guides to choir training methods have already been written (see Appendix 7), what follows now will be confined to general hints and suggestions on the broader and all-embracing aspects of choir training, the sum total of which will demand much of the choirmaster if he is to achieve lasting results.

Such things as common sense and the importance of tact in dealing with people of all ages will be considered. The relevance of a number of subsidiary aspects, such as discipline, team work and general attitudes of mind in running a choir will also be discussed as seen in their relationship to the whole. The practical success of many first-rate choir trainers has often been impaired by their inability to deal with choir members as human beings, whether it be in or out of choir.

The function of any choir, be it cathedral or village church

Their prime job in church is a simple one—to lead the worship by participating in worship themselves. If a choir is just a collection of people who come to church primarily to sing and be looked at in their uniforms, there is something radically wrong.

Much—but by no means all—of the work of a *cathedral* choir is to provide the best and most beautiful music (in its own right) as an aid or stimulus to worship. The resources of most cathedrals make this immediately more practicable than in all but a few parish churches—and, for different reasons. In *parish churches,* although the ideal should be the same, the stress will be on corporate worship, which means corporate singing, instead of the silent worship of a cathedral congregation uplifted, we hope, by the most beautiful of sounds.

In parish churches the operative word is TOGETHER, and in this the main function of the choir is to lead, but due regard must of necessity be paid for the need for every self-respecting choir regularly to perform music on its own. It is as wrong for a parish choir to ape a cathedral choir as it would be for a cathedral to try to turn itself into a parish church.

What is so often forgotten is the fact that the standard of performance of any church choir is of necessity projected on to a listening congregation. That is why the efforts of a fourth-rate choir are a positive hindrance to worship. The reverse is also true. Choirmasters must be constantly aware of the fact that it is so easy for standards to drop without their realising it. More of this later. This is one of the prices we pay for the repetitive nature of our services.

If a church is affiliated to the R.S.C.M., it is unwise to refuse a visit by a Special Commissioner. As an outsider, he has no axe to grind and is the more likely to see the faults—and the virtues —of a choir's performance.

The choirmaster's approach

So much of the ultimate success of any choir does depend on the way in which the choirmaster sets about his tasks. He must of necessity regard his work of training the choir as being as important as that of playing the organ, if not more so. He must be prepared from the outset to raise his sights very high—and keep them there. The ideal choirmaster will coax and inspire his choir, knowing when to call them to account and when to praise them. He must never let his sense of values become distorted and he must always try to be impartial in his assessments. He must plan his rehearsals so that first things come first; having worked out a plan of action, he must keep to it. He must be aware of any particular aspect of the choir's work which needs constantly to be rehearsed; it is always a good thing to work at one particular aspect and emphasise it until it has become instilled into the singers.

A choirmaster must learn to accept the limitations—vocal and mental—of his choir members; he must not think that impatience, sarcasm or even sheer bad temper will improve matters. Encouragement and a happy all round atmosphere is much more likely to produce real results.

In all things a choirmaster (if he has his wits about him), will learn by experience. When he makes his first contacts with a choir, shyness and uncertainty may understandably be evident and the choir will be quick to detect these things. It is as he begins to gain in experience that he will learn how to cope with the awkward men and women who habitually find a niche in church choirs. It is equally certain that everything ultimately depends on, and stems from, the choirmaster's natural ability and his sense of being able to "put it across".

In his early days he should watch experienced choirmasters at work and learn from them. The young organist is, for the obvious reason that he is inexperienced, generally much more proficient as an organist than he is as a choir-trainer.

Simple hints on some of the basic fundamentals of choir training

In most country parishes, many of the refinements of choir training are little more than pipe dreams. Merely to persuade a tough group of village boys and girls to sing together and make respectable sounds is in itself an achievement.

There are certain essential points which need to be constantly hammered home:

1. The production of *natural* sounds through simple basic methods of voice production. Much nonsense is frequently uttered by those whose "theories" are merely a cover for their lack of practical knowledge on the subject. Singing effortlessly and looking happy (the last thing that most people do when in church), are but a couple of simple but effective points for departure.

2. A sense of rhythm and phrasing, of words as well as of music.

3. Clarity of enunciation.

4.—and by no means least important, listening to each other and to the organ.

With the material which is available, these four fundamentals will keep most choirmasters busy for much of the time. Many are the other refinements of good choral singing but a choir must learn to walk before it can run. Unfortunately some choirs never appear to get much further than the crawling stage—and a slow crawl at that.

A choir should always be thought of, and be taught to consider itself, as an ensemble, never as a collection of individualists. The ideal of a team and all that it implies must ever be uppermost in the minds of its members; no one is too old to learn unless of course he has convinced himself that from the start he knows all the answers.

Choir members do not always genuinely appreciate the sounds they may be making when singing. It is on occasions such as this that the expertise—and often the tact—of the choirmaster will be put to the test. One of the worst, and often most painful aspects of the work of many choirs is the inability of the altos, tenors and basses to read music with any accuracy. In such instances a good treble line often covers up a multitude of sins.

How to plan a practice to the best advantage

At one end of the scale there is the choirmaster who, in general terms, aimlessly ambles through a rehearsal. In the process the choir may well have sung through most of the hymns and psalms for the coming Sunday, but it is doubtful whether they will have been taught anything constructive; it is even doubtful if, in such circumstances, mistakes will have always been corrected.

This sort of thing, which goes under the name of a choir practice, is a waste of everyone's time and energies. Any discerning singer subjected to such slipshod attitudes will, with good reason, soon transfer his loyalties to another choir or give up choir work altogether. The simple fact is that any choir under such circumstances will be bored or apathetic, the more so if the organist takes the so-called rehearsal glued to the organ stool and passing what comments he may have to make with his back to the choir.

At the other end of the scale is the choirmaster who has the rehearsal carefully planned out in advance. How he decides to do this will be the result of experience; he will know how to vary it as occasion demands and he will be able to apply a measure of flexibility without any loss of essentials. In any case, a well ordered approach will react favourably on the choir and the rehearsal will get away to a good start.

The wise choirmaster will put priorities above personal preferences. Hymns and psalms, the "bread and butter" part of the job, will be dealt with *first*. A good "sing" at the start of a rehearsal gets the muscular system working and at once produces a sense of doing something. He will not waste time rehearsing more than is necessary but correctness of notes, intonation, enunciation and punctuation must all receive due attention. It is useful to concentrate on one or two particular details over which the choir may be currently slack. If, for example, they are singing the hymn "O come, all ye Faithful", the chances are that the trebles will put in the familiar but incorrect passing note and sing

instead of

This is but one small instance of the sort of thing which must be dealt with.

If the rehearsal is meant to last for an hour, keep to it unless the circumstances, either way, are exceptional. By varying and contrasting the sequence of events in a rehearsal the attention and the interest of the choir is more likely to be retained.

Too much continually loud singing will tire a choir while an overdose of soft singing can produce flatness, as incidentally can lack of ventilation. The moral of this is to sense when the attention of the choir begins to falter and then to move on to something entirely fresh. Similarly, if a choir sounds tense, say something which will make them laugh; this helps to ventilate the lungs and causes them to relax. Most choirs sing best when standing up; this means standing up and not propping up the stalls. Even so, again for variety, allow the choir to do some of their singing sitting down—as long as they sit upright.

Never waste time at rehearsals through unnecessary talking. Choirmasters who delight in the sound of their own voices would do well to remember that people join choirs in order to sing and that the greater part of the rehearsal time should be spent in doing just that.

A businesslike approach is important; it is also infectious, for the degree of self-discipline which the choirmaster either puts, or fails to put, into his task will be quickly reflected in the work of the choir. A vital rehearsal, brimming with activity from start to finish (and that includes the necessity for having all the music ready beforehand) will communicate something to the choir in an unforgettable way. They will then go home feeling they have learned something and that the evening was perhaps more personally rewarding than the latest thriller they missed on the television.

Choir discipline

The turnout and behaviour of a choir, both in rehearsal and at service, will very largely determine its degree of musical efficiency. Any group of singers who talk loudly and incessantly in the vestry and then proceed to shuffle into the stalls, is devoid of the essence of corporate discipline and will seldom produce anything of value when it commences to sing.

Every aspect of worship—if it is to be reverent—must be offered in the best and most orderly way possible. Choir members, whether robed or not, must look tidy. Cassocks and gowns ought to be kept cleaned and in good repair. Surplices often need much more frequent laundering than they generally receive and any self-respecting choir will see to it that means are found for this to be done. If there is no fairy godmother at hand the P.C.C. must be prepared to foot the laundry bill.

To an onlooker (and a choir is usually very much in evidence) a sense of movement in processing, together with such simple things as how they stand collectively or hold their copies, will either tell of a disciplined and well trained unanimity or, as is sometimes the case, of careless apathy. Some thought, plus a lot of practice, will produce a presentable array, once a choir has learned to walk steadily in pairs rather than waddle haphazardly like ducks; (this looks especially bad from behind)!

In churches where it is the custom to bow to the altar, it is far better if the entire choir turns to the altar and bows when they have arrived in the stalls and again immediately before they leave. This is less fussy and certainly far more orderly than each pair bowing separately with the last two or three pairs almost forced to run in order to catch up with the rest of the procession. Another important point worth remembering is that an organist, like everyone else, ought to stand for the Creed.

Another sign of a well-ordered choir is the use of music lists giving *all* the necessary information for each Sunday. The blank forms, published at a very reasonable price by the R.S.C.M., are admirable; they are much to be preferred to odd scraps of paper with the hymn numbers jotted down on them. It is helpful to display a list of the music in the church porch; it provides information for the congregation and also gives the visitor some idea of the musical set up.

As in so many things concerning church music, much of what is done—or not done—in these respects, is a reasonably safe indication of the choirmaster's personal attitude and the value he places on these things. If he is by nature tidy, he will make it his business to see that the choirstalls and vestry are kept tidy. This applies also to the organ console. On visiting any church for the first time, one can usually get a very reliable inkling of the orderliness of the musical scene by taking a glance at the choirstalls. Many a beautiful chancel is rendered less beautiful when choir books and music are left haphazardly all over the place, together with an accumulation of old service papers, sweet wrappings, discarded handkerchiefs, and the odd cough lozenge. Such things are the telltale signs of an undisciplined, and therefore bad, choir.

At the present time we are, to our national shame, witnessing little insistence on the established codes of discipline and personal behaviour and this attitude is reflected wholesale in churchgoing. Consciously, or otherwise, it is only too obvious that reverence is in many instances not what it ought to be. The sense of awe which should be an important ingredient of worship will only be instilled by teaching and example.

Punctuality

As a nation we are steadily becoming more and more lax over this. Much of it is an attitude of mind thrust upon us by circumstances. Nowadays, trains are notoriously late, traffic jams are an ever present hazard and most of us try to crowd far too much into every day. The result generally is that if any one thing runs late, everything else gets out of step. This is one of the prices we pay for progress.

In the more placid life of the Church there ought to be little reason or excuse for unpunctuality. Everything, be it a service or a rehearsal, should begin at the stated time and all concerned should make it their business to arrive with time enough to spare so as to get through any preparatory jobs which need doing. A parson or organist seen rushing around the chancel lighting candles or putting out music half a minute before the service is due to start is only helping to foster the man-in-the-street's conception of the Church as something thoroughly disorganised and unbusinesslike—a state of affairs too often a reality.

To any choirmaster with a sense of punctuality, those members of a choir who drift in to rehearsal in ones and twos, anything up to fifteen minutes late (with or without excuse or apology), ensure the rehearsal getting off to a bad start in every way. It is the more annoying to all concerned when latecomers are frequently those who live the nearest and are usually, as fate will have it, the voices in short supply. All of us have experienced and contributed to the sigh of relief when the solitary tenor finally arrives and the choir is complete.

What to work for as a goal

Above all else, always aim for a high standard of performance and make your choir aware of the need for maintaining standards *at all times.*

Next in importance to this is the need for rhythmic awareness and vitality. With rhythm all around us and virtually thrust at us today through every conceivable medium, whether we wish for it or not, it is the more surprising that much of the music heard in church is so lifeless and lacking in this basic element.

It may be that the dice are heavily loaded against church music being rhythmic; most English organs, with their preponderance of wholly romantic sounds, are not by nature the most obviously rhythmic of instruments nor are they always played in a rhythmic way. Many of the hymns we sing as part of the basic diet of church music could seldom be described as alive with rhythmic interest, though much obviously depends on how they are sung—and played. This is sometimes linked to the solid and uneventful

Victorian style of singing hymns, a tradition which lingers on, rather more than intermittently, in many parishes.

Other points to consider when thinking in terms of targets for achievement, are the virtues and discipline of doing well in small things such as Amens, said or sung, and responses. It is here that the weakness and slackness of choirs is so often shown up. A tape recorder, used in discreet doses, is a very useful corrective. It tells its own tale and permits offenders in a choir the experience of hearing for themselves some of the things a choirmaster may have been complaining about for a long time.

An individual ought never to be singled out for criticism in front of the whole choir. By speaking to the offender privately the chances are that he will resent any comments far less than if he is called to account in front of his colleagues. Such collective remarks as "Basses, you are dragging" are pointless if the criticism is in fact being directed at one person. Although the person concerned may be blissfully unaware of the fact that he is being got at, the rest of the basses will appreciate only too quickly the object of the comment.

In the final count it must be remembered that none of us relishes criticism, even though we know it to be justifiable.

Giving responsibility to members of the choir, especially the younger ones, provides them with an added sense of purpose in doing something which is both useful and productive with something to show at the end of it. There are many jobs in this category, ranging from being "Organ boy" (and learning, often by bitter experience, the need to find the correct hymns and psalms), to being responsible for discipline in the vestry. These tasks may in themselves seem small but they help to provide a sound basis both for character-training and for adult life, quite apart from ensuring that the wheels run more smoothly.

An important feature of choir work, as in anything demanding collectivity, is that of instilling into the members the need for a team spirit. This is not always easy to achieve, especially in what is a very mixed bunch who meet once or twice a week and whose ages may well range from seven to seventy, or even eighty. Nevertheless, a choir is a team and the successful team is one in which the group works together as a group, no matter what the propensities of the individuals may be.

A choir in which there is a rigid demarcation between children and adults, or between the choirmaster and the singers, is never likely to be a really happily contented group. An experienced choirmaster with a knowledge of human behaviour knows just how far he can become friendly with his choir without a loss of authority or respect. The degree to which this can be taken is likely to vary through circumstances between any two choirs.

The difficulties of maintaining a week by week standard

Most choirs can make the necessary effort to mount the occasional recital successfully; it is in the round of Sunday services, with their inevitable element of repetitiveness and familiarity, that problems arise and choirs tend to become careless.

A choirmaster must always and insistently keep his singers up to the mark, especially over finer points such as said Amens and neat standing, sitting and kneeling. The business of processing is likely to be a constant headache to any choirmaster who rightly believes in, and insists on, its importance.

In order to achieve any continuing standard in routine work, be it singing, deportment or general standards of behaviour, the choirmaster must constantly be aware of the inescapable fact that choir practices must be an interesting occasion to which all will look forward with keen anticipation.

Making choir practices interesting

Ideally, every choir practice should be vital and buzzing with interest and activity from start to finish. If a rehearsal misfires, the choirmaster must ask himself why this is so. Is it because of him? He must constantly review his conduct of rehearsals, be self-critical and always put himself in the place of the recipient and remember that everything a choir does will, in greater or lesser degree, reflect his training and his influence over them.

Rehearsals should be well planned in advance. Never, on any account, should a choirmaster stand meandering and dithering in front of the choir, while deciding what to do next. Worst of all, he must never waste valuable time making up his mind which chant or tune to use. The unbusinesslike attitude of working things out as one goes along merely reflects a careless attitude of mind which will quickly cause the choir to become restless and bored, quite apart from the practical annoyance of wasting everyone's time.

In the matter of taking rehearsals, the choirmaster can often profit from the example of his cathedral organist, watching him, whenever possible, in action. Most cathedral organists have far too little rehearsal time to deal with everything which ought to be rehearsed. As a result, every available minute has to be utilised. Fifty minutes of highly charged non-stop rehearsal will keep any choir on its toes and combine to produce some results, be it in the humblest of village churches or in the best of cathedrals. In either instance, these results will not be achieved without considerable preparation nor without the willingness of the choir to go along with the choirmaster.

With experience, both personal and in assessing the capabilities of a choir, one eventually learns what to rehearse and what to leave. Even so, it is possible to be caught out from time to time. Both choirmaster and choir ought, at the end of a rehearsal, to be healthily tired; if not, all concerned cannot have been working and concentrating really hard.

Rehearse at regular times on regular days. Never alter this, or cut practices short, unless there is a very good reason for doing so. On the other hand, a choir which has worked hard for some special service—which in the event has gone well—will appreciate the next rehearsal ending a quarter of an hour earlier than usual.

A choir, unless it is composed of very unusual people, will respond to—and catch something of the choirmaster's devotion to the task in hand. Time and again I have seen the work of the slovenly choirmaster reflected in the singing of his choir.

Above all, maintain a sense of humour and an understanding of human nature. Dull rehearsals with little sense of direction achieve equally little result. Always have something *new* to work at, no matter how simple, and always try to encourage the sense of having done at least some things well. Every choir practice should add something positive to the standard of the singing. Through the choirmaster, the choir must learn to cultivate an awareness of what constitutes good singing and bad singing. He should praise the choir when praise is due and curse them when cursing is due.

In the end it can be seen that everything ultimately depends on the choirmaster. His influence, for good or bad, will be paramount and immediately obvious to the most casual of observers. The measure of achievement in good choirs is a reflection of the skill, musicianship and personality of the person in charge. Similarly, untidy and half-hearted singing will in equal measure stem from the attitude of mind generated by the choirmaster. This in its turn will produce the added hindrance of poor attendance at weekly rehearsals. When this happens one often wonders if the choirmaster is aware of the harm he is doing to the cause of the Church.

Four final points of emphasis for choirmasters:

1. First of all get the notes and time values correct, *then* move on to musical refinements. If you say "We'll go through that again" you must explain why. Merely to sing something a second time without endeavouring to better it is a waste of everyone's time. Once a choir has really learnt something well, they will not easily forget it.

2. Teach one thing at a time and teach it thoroughly.

3. Choir training is basically "personnel management". You show them what to do but *they* do it.

4. A very important fact which ought always to be borne in mind when underlying all the previous remarks is that singing, to all intents and purposes, is a choir's only medium of expression.

7 Organ playing

> To Protestants (organ music) acts as a very real help in finding their way from the world's level to that level which worship is designed to bring them, especially when it is the first thing they hear as they come into church.
>
> *Erik Routley:* WORDS, MUSIC AND THE CHURCH

We need little reminder that much of our traditional way of life in England is, in so many ways, undergoing radical change. This current course of events is altering and even, in some instances, undermining the structure of our society. This process of change threatens (and this is often to the good) much of what has been comfortably established in the Church as tradition. More will be said of this later.

Arising to some extent from present day circumstances is the acute shortage of organists. This rightly gives cause for much concern if only for the practical restrictions it imposes. There are a number of contributory reasons for this, some of which will be discussed in the course of this book. Factors such as the frequently unrealistic rates of remuneration, in many cases pathetically out of all proportion to the cost of living today, together with the difficulties of finding—and keeping—choir members, are but two of the factors impeding the progress of church music at the present time.

These are very real problems which deter many from becoming regular organists while many who do valiantly struggle on Sunday by Sunday, often against heavy odds, are in no small way disheartened. Perhaps the writing is on the wall for all who have eyes to see?

As a result of this shortage, the local "organist" is often not an organist and is recruited simply because there is no one else capable of playing at all. But for him—or her—the organ would be silent on Sundays. All praise then to the invaluable work many of these people do even if much of their effort is largely a question of groping in the dark, for many are virtually untrained and would be the first to admit it.

What follows is some attempt to point the way by providing organists with some fundamental help as a start.

BASIC TECHNIQUE

It is essential to obtain a good grounding in the fundamental technique of organ playing, nor is it difficult to obtain this if one goes about it in the right way. It is amazing how high a standard can be achieved by amateur organists though the end products do tend to vary very much.

The important thing is to go to a good teacher for help even if, at the end of it all, you do not feel yourself to be as proficient as you would wish. You will at least be on the right track. For all of us, bad habits are only too easily acquired, often without our realising it. Bad habits once acquired are exceedingly difficult to dispose of. The discipline imposed on us by a first rate teacher can help, in no small measure, to improve our contribution to the services.

FINGER TECHNIQUE

Because the organ is a wind instrument and because the sound stops immediately a note ceases to be depressed, it is generally assumed (and often by those who ought to know better) that a continuous *legato* style must of necessity always form the basis of organ technique. This is only a half truth and a dangerous assertion in that it leads to the endless unphrased "*legato* at all costs" style which gives the organ the reputation of being a dull instrument. Just think for one moment of the effect of always adopting an uncompromising *legato* when playing a string or wind instrument.

Add to this the inherent difficulties of coping with the heavy

19th century tracker action which is a feature of many English organs and we start heaping up endless problems. The very nature of organ technique (not to mention the added distraction of having to use feet as well as hands) implies the necessity for an entirely different approach from that of playing a keyboard instrument such as the piano. Mistakes are the more easily exposed and there is no sustaining pedal to cover up a multitude of blemishes. Because of this the organ is merciless in exposing untidy and inaccurate playing.

RHYTHM AND PHRASING

Because we tend to be immersed with the mechanics of playing the organ, such as the manipulation of stops and changing manuals, we often overlook these two primary ingredients without which any performance on any instrument lacks musicianship and interest. Rhythm and phrasing are the more important when we consider the way in which organ sounds are produced. Because of the lack of so-called "touch" and tone control, as in the piano, organ phrasing needs to be given a top priority all the time.

HOW TO PRACTISE

It never seems to occur to many teachers how important it is to teach their pupils *how* to practise. A little guidance in this respect can pay handsome dividends as most people, left to their own initiative, have little idea of how to set about the business of practising, though they may well spend many hours, to little avail, at the console. A teacher, by bringing his accumulated experience to bear, can guide and advise a pupil so that over a period of time, the pupils can ultimately assimilate the role of the teacher, but with his own experience behind him as a yardstick.

Some points on practising

1. Practise *regularly*. A small amount of regular practise will, in most instances, produce better results than long bouts of spasmodic playing when concentration so easily lapses.

2. Learn *slowly*. Always pin-point errors at once; see why they are errors (it will often be fingering), isolate them and then work out how to correct them, once and for all.

3. Pedal technique is alien to a keyboard player. Concentration of this aspect is therefore the more important. It presents many recurring problems and you must not expect a quick return for your labours. Organ playing is made untidy and unrhythmic when the feet move reluctantly and out of step with the hands. (See Appendix 8 for suggested books on organ technique, etc).

4. Do not always necessarily begin practising at bar one of the piece you are working at. Make it a firm rule sometimes to begin half way through. The first section of a piece is, for this reason, often much better known than subsequent pages.

5. Always aim for a high standard by being over critical of your efforts, and aim, at the end of a period of practising, at seeing some results and, above all, some improvement in accuracy and confidence.

Because of the nature of the work of being a church organist with its necessary repetitiveness week by week, it is so easy to get into the bad habits mentioned earlier, let alone a rut—and without realising it. This can be especially real if an organist lives in a country area and, rightly or wrongly, feels himself to be cut off from musical activity in the bigger towns. If, as should be the case with all of us, he has doubts about his playing, he should seek the advice of his cathedral organist or some other person qualified to help. He must never fight shy of asking the advice of such people; part of their job is to help other organists and in the majority of instances, although a cathedral organist may not be able to give regular tuition, the chances are that he will be glad to give advice and possibly a consultation lesson now and again.

An organist should be constantly on the lookout for help, seeking reasoned and qualified advice, (there are always plenty of quacks ready to give their unwanted opinions on every conceivable church music matter), while never failing to take any advantage which may come his way to sit in the organ loft at a cathedral and watch the organist play for a service.

Above all else, *he must always aim at a high standard.* There are, unfortunately, far too many organists interested almost exclusively in specifications, wind pressures and "nicking" rather than in the fundamental business of playing the organ and of improving existing standards. Organists' Associations, which ought ideally to be geared to helping in this way, so often degenerate into little more than groups of narrow-minded busybodies whose only interest is to spend Saturday afternoon, *en masse,* "trying" organs. If only some of the energy—and expense—involved in driving around the countryside in this pursuit were channelled into some organ lessons, the average standard of performance among many amateur organists might improve considerably.

CORRECT USE OF STOPS

The possibilities which an organ offers in the way of registration are seldom exploited to the full. Even with a small one manual instrument minus pedals, a considerable tonal variety can be obtained in a number of ways:

1. Playing the right hand an octave higher than written.

2. The use of single stops.

3. Playing without pedals; (this can be a most welcome relief). If there is an 8 ft. flute, it can be used to advantage on its own for a change. Excessive and prolonged use of 16 ft. pedal tone, especially the inevitable and generally characterless Bourdon, quickly become monotonous; it also thickens up the texture of the music far too much.

4. If there are two or more manuals they should not always, as a matter of habit, be coupled together. On far too few occasions are the Great flutes or diapasons heard on their own.

5. Playing with the swell box either closed or open. This avoids the almost magnetic lure of mechanically opening and closing the swell box without any real regard for the demands of the music. Such indiscriminate "pumping" of the swell pedal with

the right foot is often made the substitute for phrasing and expression while the left foot manages the pedalling as best it can. The distance between pedal notes more than a tone apart makes it a physical impossibility to play smoothly when using only the left foot.

6. Whenever possible, families of stops should be used together rather than *ad hoc* mixing of flutes and strings. They do not always blend, especially if a string stop happens to be keenly voiced.

7. To add brightness to the tone, do not automatically draw stops of 8 ft., 4 ft. and 2 ft. pitch. The use of 8 ft. and 2 ft. stops gives a bright and clean sound which is in distinct contrast to the sound produced when a 4 ft. stop is included.

8. If there is a 16 ft. manual stop, experiment by using it on its own but played an octave higher.

INCORRECT USE OF STOPS

1. The habit of playing the pedal part an octave lower than written is one of the most common faults to be encountered in organ playing; it immediately produces a cloying thickness to the texture and only serves to cover up any rhythmic vitality. It can, on occasion, such as in the last verse of a hymn, provide an effective contrast when tastefully employed in *small* doses.

2. If an organ has 16 ft. manual stops, especially of the Bourdon or Diapason type, their use in company with other stops, *when playing without pedals,* produces one of the worst excesses of muddy and unmusical sound.

3. If there is a Twelfth, use it together with the Fifteenth. On its own, as the highest pitched stop, the texture is distorted by the predominance of the vulnerable fifth above the fundamental.

4. Be sparing in the use of Mixtures. Their effect is especially penetrating when used to excess but is colourful when used in small doses.

The wise organist will do a lot of experimenting with registration. He will vary the stops all he can but will always find out for himself how it sounds in the body of the church before he actually tries it out on the unsuspecting congregation. The effect will often be surprisingly different from what is heard at the console, so it is useful to get someone to play while the organist judges for himself the effect in the body of the church. Sounds, which to the organist at the console, may be charming, could be unbearable to the congregation.

The drabness of an almost unvaried and unimaginative *mezzo forte* which some organists rely on, cannot be calculated to inspire either choir or congregation. An organist should also remember that the chances are that he is likely to play far too loudly, often —perhaps—without realising it. If in any doubt, he should ask the members of the congregation—that is, if they do not volunteer the information! If the organist has a discerning wife she will quickly tell him the error of his ways in this and other respects. He must never be misled by thinking that the louder he plays the more he will be inspiring the choir and congregation to sing; it is more likely that it will completely put them off and that they will give up in despair. Rhythmic and vital organ playing, based on a foundation of diapason tone, will be more calculated to bring the best out of them.

Now and again, if at all possible, he should sit in the congregation and get someone to play for a service. If he really wants to, he will learn more from this than from anything. The results might be quite enlightening.

ACCOMPANYING THE SERVICES—WITH OR WITHOUT A CHOIR

> His primary task is to accompany the singing in such a way that the singers will be inspired to interpret the words in the spirit of true worship; of self-glorification there must be none. He must have sympathy with the singers: he must coax and not drive them.
>
> *Gerald H. Knight:* TWENTY QUESTIONS ON CHURCH MUSIC

One cannot stress too much the importance which attaches to this aspect of the work for the accompanying of the services is the "bread and butter" of any church organist.

He must be ready to size up the difference between leading and accompanying and be able to switch from one to the other at a moment's notice. His approach should, in any event, be designed to giving a lead to corporate singing and be contrived in such a way as to support the congregation—and perhaps the choir—without ever appearing obtrusive. At its ideal, accompanying provides a mere background. How one puts this into action will, in the end, do much to set or mar in no uncertain way the pattern of worship. The onus laid upon the organist is therefore great; not only skill but sympathy and taste is needed. All this can be achieved if approached in the right way.

If a church has no choir at all or only very inadequate forces, the organist must be more alert than ever and above all else rhythmic, which means that his playing must be alive and, as occasion demands, almost dancelike.

HYMNS

The first thing to remember—something which is often disregarded—is that not every hymn goes at the same speed or with virtually the same degree of monotonous *mezzo forte,* with the final verse, irrespective of the meaning of the words, always much louder.

Pace is to a great extent determined by the words; a hymn of praise is likely to move more quickly than a penitential hymn in a minor key, though there will be exceptions to this. The words should most certainly determine registration, though some of the extravagances of sentimental word painting which derive from Victorian days should be swiftly dispensed with. One of the best known examples comes at the end of A. and M. 27: "in life" (loud)—"in death" (very soft) re-echoes something of the hushed and almost sinister preoccupation with the idea of death as seen through the sentimentally clouded eyes of the 19th century. To sing these words in this way verges on to the province of the music hall.

Now for some general hints to organists on playing hymns:

1. All hymn playing should be underlined by an uncompromising rhythmic vitality.

2. A hymn *must* of necessity be announced at the same speed at which it is intended to be sung. This is the main reason for

playing over a tune. It follows that a big *rallentando* at the end of the play-over destroys any rhythmic pulse which may have been set.

3. Hymns should be played exactly as they are written. No one has the right to add any notes to what appears on the printed page. The addition of dominant sevenths is considered by many organists to be fair game. If the composer of the tune *Franconia* wanted

he would have written it instead of

4. There should be a tidy attack and release to the start and end of each verse, therefore be sure *all* the notes go down and come off together.

5. Sing the words to yourself as you play. In this way, you are more likely, in your playing, to play according to the meaning of the words you are supposed to be accompanying.

6. If pauses are to be observed at the ends of lines, they must have a definite length, be consistent and rhythmically in the pulse already set for the music. In *English Hymnal* 533, the second line of *Nun Danket* is written as

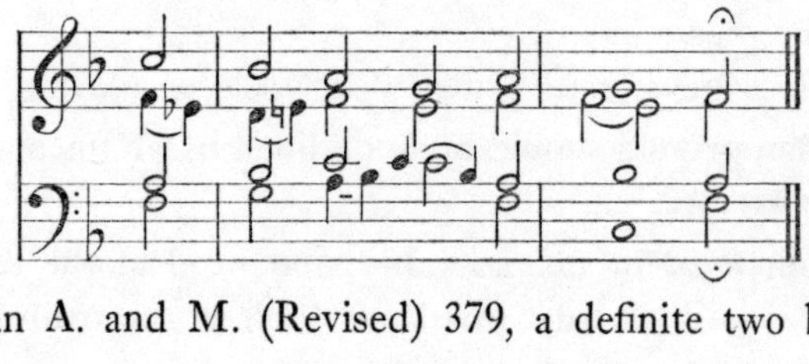

whereas in A. and M. (Revised) 379, a definite two beat note replaces the vague pause which could be interpreted as being of any length:

7. As a general rule, be sure that any long notes which may occur during the course of a hymn are given full value. Count them out in strict, unhurried, time. Conversely, carry over the ends of lines where there are no commas, otherwise the sense of the words is destroyed.
8. Gaps between verses ought to be consistent, allowing ample time for the singers to take breath. The organist who all but joins up one verse to the next can have little understanding of the physical aspect of singing. If he is singing to himself whilst playing, he will know the time needed to take a breath.
9. It is preferable that organist and singers begin each verse together. The habit is easily acquired and it soon makes superfluous the traditional, but quite pointless, "gathering note".
10. Amens, if sung, are the most effective when lively and rhythmic; they are far less successful when indefinite and sentimental. The use of dominant sevenths, alluded to in paragraph three is even more objectionable in Amens when

is substituted for

The indiscriminate addition of passing notes such as

Redhead No.46

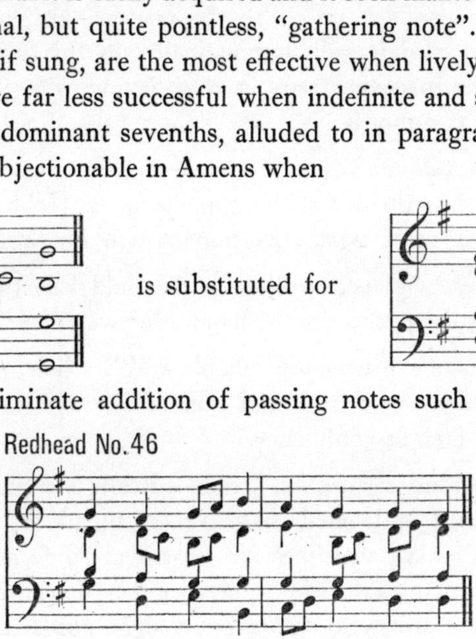

is an unwarranted presumption on the part of the organist and merely falsifies the intentions of the composer.

Other points worth remembering are:

(a) In order to mark the rhythm, detach the right hand while playing the left hand and pedals legato.

(b) Spacing of chords. Some rearrangement of what is on the printed page is often necessary as the playing of two notes in each hand is sometimes physically difficult or even impossible:

Richmond

will have to be re-distributed as

when playing without pedals.

(c) If you are using the pedals there is no need to play the bass part on the manuals (providing the manuals are coupled to the pedals). The pedals will automatically do this and the hands are then free to concentrate, in conjunction with (b) above, on spacing out the chords.

(d) Avoid a *rallentando* at the end of every verse of a hymn. It is so easy to do this without realising it. Hold it in reserve for the final verse where its impact will be the greater.

(e) Some verses played without pedals add variety, if only for the fact that the pedals are the more effective when they re-enter.

(f) If you have a reasonably reliable SATB choir, give them an unaccompanied verse here and there. This also creates variety and gives the choir confidence.

(g) Many hymns, as printed, are melodically too high, e.g. in *A. and M.* "Lord enthroned in heavenly splendour" to the tune *St Helen.* The last two lines are excessively high and the hymn is much more singable when played a tone lower in the key of B flat. As the ability to transpose at sight needs much practice before it can be done fluently, it is wiser—and safer—to write out the transposed version.

(h) Free harmonies. Used tastefully, these can bring new meaning to the words in certain places. Even more so than in transposing, this is a specialised art best used occasionally. If you decide to do this never trust on inspiration coming on the spur of the moment. Either write out what you want to do or use published examples (see Appendix 9). The golden rule *must* be never to embark on your own efforts at this sort of thing unless you can, with a clear conscience, produce something better than the original. (This is not easy!) And—always warn the choir in advance when you are going to play free harmonies.

PSALMS

The psalms provide one of the most magnificent and stimulating features of Anglican worship, the words of which are some of the most beautiful poetry to be found in the Liturgy. Unfortunately, the problems of singing the psalms are very real ones and, as such, were dealt with in Chapter 3. Also, the excessive length of many of the psalms makes them unacceptable for general worship though happily they can still be heard in their entirety in Cathedrals as set out for use on each day of the month.

In accompanying the psalms an organist ideally should know the chants from memory; this obviously helps in concentrating on the words and the pointing. Sing the words—either to yourself or audibly—as you play, always remembering that the basic rules of speech rhythm ought to apply.

In order that the psalm may be allowed to flow (and this is almost more important than anything), a light accompaniment should always be provided, avoiding the use of 16 feet manual stops or excessively heavy pedal stops. Always allow the sense of the words to determine what stops you will use; for example, Psalm 46 needs a more forceful and vigorous accompaniment than Psalm 23.

Two small but important points:

1. If the reciting note is very short, e.g.

play the chord as lightly and quickly as possible. The old idea of singing "*er*-cording to thy word" is often still very much with us.

2. When using a double chant, be ready for a "second half" but never anticipate the choir to such an extent that it is obvious to all—including the choir—that you are making sure they do not miss it.

There nearly always seems to be a diversity of opinion as to how chants should be played over. Although the note values (semibreves, minims etc.) are of course arbitrary and are dispensed with once the singing of the psalm has begun, to play over the chant with the time values as written seems much more shapely—and consistent—than the succession of vague, timeless chords we so often hear.

The choice of chant must obviously be suitable to the underlying sentiments of the words—an aspect of psalm singing not always heeded. Too often a chant is chosen because it happens to be a favourite of the organist (or the Vicar) and it has to do duty irrespective of the essential marrying of words and music. Similarly, if a change of chant is contemplated during the course of a psalm, its tonality must to some extent be in common with what has gone before. In this respect, avoid any uncomfortable jolt (see page 23).

Many of the above remarks apply equally well to the accompaniment of Merbecke. As with psalms, Merbecke can be so heavy and lifeless when accompanied unimaginatively. Various editions of Merbecke together with their virtues—or otherwise—are listed as Appendix 10.

VOLUNTARIES

> Dr. Nathaniel Micklem once said that the introductory organ music does for Protestants what the scent of incense does for Catholics; it lifts them over the threshold of the church.
>
> *Erik Routley:* WORDS, MUSIC AND THE CHURCH

Although this is in some respects secondary to service playing, it is a very important and integral part of the organist's work and should be as equally well prepared as the accompaniment of the services.

Conversely, it is unfortunate that some organists who go to great pains in preparing voluntaries can be so perfunctory as to inflict shoddy and ill prepared accompanying on choir and congregation alike. The work of any choir can be enhanced by an inspiring organ accompaniment; it can just as easily be marred by slipshod efforts on the part of the organist.

What is played before a service—and how it is played—can contribute much towards creating an atmosphere conducive to worship. Music so played as a preliminary to the Parish Communion or during the Administration can, under these conditions, be of the utmost help and significance to worshippers. Too often, alas, the organist rushes to the console a few moments ahead of the oncoming choir and proceeds to improvise, or rather "doodle", in a depressingly dull manner using, often without realising it, the few recurring clichés which he has used Sunday by Sunday for years past.

Improvising, if it is to be both convincing and musical, is an extremely difficult aspect of the organist's work. To a few it comes easily, to some less so and to others not at all. Although the ability to improvise in a musical way is a useful asset, there is no loss of face in being unable to do it. If this happens to be your lot, cheerfully accept the fact, (you will not be the only person), and play set pieces rather than inflict on the listener something inferior merely because you cannot take the trouble to prepare a piece. If you are not sure of the standard of your improvising seek the advice of someone qualified to give you a fair and constructive criticism.

All voluntaries should, as a matter of personal conscience, be as carefully chosen as they are rehearsed. If one takes the trouble to find out, it is surprising how much suitable—and often technically simple—music is available for any specific occasion. Too often the old and familiar pattern emerges of a voluntary being extracted from the cupboard during the sermon and played without any preparation, often with dire results.

Organists who ought to know better—and often would have known better in their more youthful and less slipshod days—seem to delight in the "I've not played this piece for over twenty years, but here goes" attitude. Setting about matters in this way reflects neither musicianship nor conscience nor, one would venture to suggest, a deep rooted love for one's vocation as a church organist. Such methods cannot be expected to instil a love of organ music among the members of a congregation and such playing as results from it deserves to be partnered by the conversation of an uninterested congregation intent on getting out of church by the quickest escape route possible.

Fifty years ago it might have been easier to get away with this sort of thing but today young and old alike are much more discerning; they have the right, in or out of church, to hear music as well performed as they can hear it on the radio or on records. What is more, they are likely to transfer their affections to a church where the music is presentable and worth listening to.

As a result of my experiences I have come to three general conclusions:

1. That most organists have too small a repertoire. Much of it stems from what they learned as students and they have, over the years, added little or nothing new to it.
2. Much of what they play is dated, of poor musical value and often confined to the worst excesses of Victoriana. (As an example, study the contents of the endless volumes of *Voluntaries for the Organ, American Organ or Harmonium by* Caleb Simper.)
3. The low standard of performance (borne out by the above remarks).

Again and again I am confronted with such comments as "I have no time nowadays to practise" or "I am too old to learn". If a person holds these views and uses them as excuses, why bother to continue being an organist? It all seems more than slightly hypocritical.

I am convinced that a major issue in this business of voluntaries lies in the fact that many organists scorn the use of simple music. They become mesmerised by the mere sight of a page black with notes, especially if it promises to be very loud and very fast. As a result they "attempt"—in public—music which is beyond their technical resources and is therefore inadequately performed. Many organists persist in this approach and seldom, if ever, learn the folly of their ways. We *all* have to accept our limitations; the greater the musician the more so.

Choose simple music and aim to play it really well. There is today more opportunity than ever before to assess standards in playing. Listen to first-rate organists, live or recorded, and, as mentioned on a number of occasions already, seek the advice of those best qualified to help (even if you have to pay for it). Never be fearful of asking for advice even if the truth hurts.

Choose music from all periods. Much of the organ music of the 18th century was written for manuals only, simply because very few organs at that time (certainly in England) possessed pedalboards. There is a wealth of interesting and often very lively music of all periods written for manuals only. (Appendix 11 lists some examples). Generally speaking, much of the music for manuals only is simple and very worthwhile, providing one avoids the 19th century editions which zealously filled out the chords and added pedal parts. In this respect, compare Sidney Campbell's admirable editing of the Voluntary in C minor of Maurice Green (O.U.P.) with the heavily overladen version which was the work of John E. West (Novello).

Much of this type of music needs simple registration, often single stops and very seldom the Swell to Great coupler. Aim rather for echo effects which were one of the chief means of securing variety used by composers of the 17th and 18th centuries.

It is well to remember that in music of this period the directions *Allegro* and *Vivace* mean a lively or vivacious interpretation rather than pursuing a break neck speed. In this respect it must again be emphasised that *legato* is but one aspect of organ playing. A detached and rhythmic style will help to produce the effect intended in the 18th century music, whereas most of the Romantic music of the 19th century, (Mendelssohn and Rheinberger etc.), needs a generally more legato style and use of the swell pedal because of the texture and underlying character of the music.

Coming to the 20th century there is an abundance of hymn-tune preludes, some better than others. The idea of taking someone else's tune and using it as a basis for composition has been fair game down through the centuries, though some composers have managed it better than others. (Appendix 12 lists some examples of voluntaries using pedals, which are a little more difficult than those in Appendix 11).

Finally, listen to all the music you possibly can—not only organ music—as a guide to style and phrasing. Much of the colour of orchestral music can, and should, be transferred to organ playing, for the organ is by its very nature a basically dull and mechanical instrument, simply because one's fingers cannot produce tone in the way that most other instruments can. By hearing as much "out of church" music as possible you will help to broaden your musicianship and, in the process, become a better organist.

Summing up

The accompanying of church services means that you inflict yourself—for better or worse—on a choir and congregation. In this respect, much of what you do and how you go about it will react in no uncertain way on the atmosphere of worship. Always bear in mind the responsibility this implies and because of it, do all you can to improve the standard of your playing. The lesson to be learned from tape-recording yourself and your choir is likely to be a humiliating experience but one which, in the end, will teach you as no other medium is likely to.

Do not resent criticism about your playing made in good faith by members of the congregation. You don't sit where they do and the effect may be quite different, even to the extent of being unbearable, especially in loudness, away from the organ console.

You may not be a great organist but always be trying to do the job better; therefore always be on the lookout for ways and means of improving your playing. Being critical of our efforts is not always the saving grace it ought to be.

8 How to acquire help

THE DANGERS OF BEING OUT OF TOUCH

Many organists and choirmasters are cut off, either voluntarily or by force of circumstance, though the latter is only partly valid today when means of transport are so much easier than twenty or thirty years ago.

Even so, distance is still made an excuse. It is surprising to find how many organists who go to endless trouble and expense to arrange a holiday in Spain or Italy, will think up a wide variety of excuses to justify absenting themselves from a church music event taking place a comparatively few miles away in their Cathedral or major parish church.

Environment can easily become a dangerous occupational hazard to those who work for the Church, be they clergy or laity and it is essential for an organist to be constantly in touch with all that is going on. The need for this has never been more apparent than today when so many changes are reshaping both the Liturgy and our ways of worship. These are events which none of us can afford, to our peril, to disregard, for this new thought and new look is affecting the musical content of the services in no small measure.

It cannot be stressed too frequently that because of the high standards of performance readily available on recordings and radio the public demands—and has a right to demand—a similarly high standard in the music they hear when they go to church. They seldom realise, or concern themselves with the many problems facing choirmasters today, problems which make this target virtually impossible of achievement in many parishes. The man in the pew perhaps knows little of the conflict between professional and amateur music making though we, as organists, are only too aware through practical experience of the cleavage and all that it implies.

Despite the hard facts of these realities, it must always be uppermost in our minds that, no matter how simple and fundamental our church music may be, it must be well performed at the highest possible standard, even when in the humblest village church. This fact must never escape us if we wish our music to be a truly worthy adornment to the services. We should ever remember and take comfort from the fact that most people, if they take the trouble, are capable of much higher standards of performance than they would ever credit themselves with. This is one of the most exciting aspects of amateur music-making.

THE NEED TO GAIN AS MUCH KNOWLEDGE AS POSSIBLE

Organists and choirmasters seem, in the main, to be divided into two main categories:

(1) Those who are unduly meek or even self-derogatory concerning their own ability, and

(2) Those who think they know all the answers. These are the most dangerous group and often the most impossible to deal with. They are, for instance, unlikely to read this book. They are sure to resent any help from anyone, though it may well be that they are inwardly aware of their shortcomings and, because of this, assume an air of arrogance and resentfulness towards anyone who may venture—with justification—to point out their obvious deficiences. People such as this are, if one has even the opportunity of any dealings with them, almost impossible to reason with.

Every organist and choirmaster should view as an essential part of his work the continual acquiring of knowledge. In this way he will be enabled by every means at his disposal, to do his work with a much higher degree of skill and confidence than would otherwise be possible.

He should digest all the relevant literature he can lay hands on. From a personal point of view it is always preferable to work with some objective in mind; as a yardstick of personal achievement and of assessing standards, the Associated Board examinations in organ playing are very useful, whatever one's age may be. As a choirmaster, one can take The Archbishop of Canterbury's Certificate in church music and for diploma holders of the Royal College of Organists, the Choir Training Diploma (CHM).

Organists' Associations are a mixed blessing and seldom achieve much more than a meeting ground for organists discussing "shop". Experience often shows that when an enlightened committee plans lectures or instructional meetings, such events seldom draw many of the members who prefer to spend a Saturday afternoon rushing round the countryside engaged in the pursuits mentioned in the previous chapter. (See Appendix 13 for suggested books to help in service playing).

ORGAN LESSONS

The older one becomes, the more important it is to have continual refreshers, yet only a handful of organists seem to feel the need for this and so take steps to do something about it. The plea usually put forward is either lack of time or the pointless remark that "you can't teach an old dog new tricks". As a result, the congregation (and the choir) have to suffer the old dog's bad habits while the old dog, in his turn, wonders why so few of the congregation show much enthusiasm or appreciation for his playing.

In point of fact, one is *never* too old to learn.

The playing of voluntaries is only one part of the church organist's work. Much more important, and of greater influence, is efficiency in accompanying hymns and psalms. Doing this well, or not, affects the entire church. A congregation can—and often does—escape the voluntary but must endure what the organist does during the service.

How often does an organist ask for lessons in accompanying?

For some obscure reason, this seems to be thought of as something which looks after itself compared with what the average organist considers to be the more important business of playing pieces. This attitude puts the cart before the horse in no uncertain way. An organist is appointed to a church primarily to accompany the services, not to give recitals. The prevailing low standards of accompanying in many churches (and in my experience much of it is deplorably bad) would uncover some very considerably chinks in the armour.

I have tried the experiment of inviting four or five organists to spend a couple of hours together with me during which we all play to each other and, in an informal atmosphere, freely criticise each other. I would venture to suggest that in this way much can be achieved, especially through the process of listening to each other.

THE ROYAL SCHOOL OF CHURCH MUSIC

One of the best means of help is that provided by the R.S.C.M. No choir is too bad nor P.C.C. too poor to become affiliated. The R.S.C.M. is in existence to help choirs to improve their standards though one finds, again and again, that people are not aware of what the R.S.C.M. is doing all over the world to help in these difficult days.

The principles of the R.S.C.M. (see Appendix 14) together with the facilities offered (Appendix 15) are, or should be, a ready made yardstick for all concerned with the Church and its music. R.S.C.M. policy, which is the result of many years' practical experience, can be of immense help not only to the humblest village organist but also to the grandest Cathedral musicians. Yet, despite this, there is still unfortunately a minority climate of opinion which often stubbornly fights shy of affiliation, mistakenly interpreting it as a type of Trade Union in which you have to conform to the party line. Choirs join the R.S.C.M. because they wish to be associated with the work for which it stands and because they feel the need for help. Affiliated choirs who are anxious to better their performance voluntarily undertake "to do their best to promote the cause of good church music and in this to be guided by the principles and recommendations set forth by the R.S.C.M.".

The R.S.C.M. was founded in 1927 by Sir Sydney Nicholson who was at the time organist at Westminster Abbey. From the start it set out to be "a church society working for the encouragement of good church music". It believes that only the best of which we are capable is good enough for the worship of Almighty God.

What are the benefits of affiliation? "What do we get out of it"? Its work is divided into four main channels, three of which concern us here. The fourth branch, that of training full time students for the profession, takes place at its headquarters at Addington Palace in Surrey. Organists and choirs can derive much benefit from what is offered:

1. Instructional Courses

An impressive annual list of residential courses of varying length, for choirboys, choirgirls, organists and choirmasters. These courses are held either at Addington Palace or at centres throughout the country. There are also one day and even half-day schools arranged locally in the various Dioceses. In these events, up to sixty boys and girls work under expert guidance at the "bread and butter" essentials of choir work. Versicles and responses, psalms, canticles and hymns for the basis of the instruction and the day's work usually concludes with the singing of Evensong.

These courses provide much food for thought, and experience shows that, as a result, choir members and organists return to their routine work healthily stimulated and with a fresh outlook. A number of P.C.C.s help financially towards the cost of sending some of their musicians on these courses and have found that it is money well spent.

2. Publications

A major part of R.S.C.M. policy is the publication of choir music. Much of this, including specially commissioned new works, is produced in very reasonably priced collections under one cover. The advantages of having music for special occasions in one book need hardly be stressed; the wide range of available publications includes music for the Church's seasons, Holy Communion and Weddings as well as a wide choice of music for Choral Festivals, Diocesan or otherwise.

R.S.C.M. News, an informative quarterly booklet, is sent free to all affiliated choirs together with the pamphlet *Promoting Church Music. English Church Music,* published annually in May, is an up-to-the-minute collection of articles and reviews embracing a wide variety of thought and opinion which should be of real concern to all serious students of church music. There is also an informative series of *Study Notes* which range through a variety of practical subjects such as *Chanting for Beginners, Conducting for Church Musicians* and *The Parish Church Organ.* All are written by experts in each particular field.

Recordings, Christmas cards, choristers' diaries, music filing boxes, service sheets and various badges are but a few of the useful publications also available. Affiliated choirs are allowed 50 per cent discount on most of what is available.

3. Advice

This, together with practical help on every aspect of church music is to be had on request. Qualified church musicians, many of them highly experienced and eminent, help, as Special Commissioners, to further the work of the R.S.C.M. They are available as requested to visit choirs in their own churches. The personal contact thus made is a useful process for providing help and encouragement and is followed up by a frank but constructively helpful report on all aspects of the choir's work.

Those of us who try to help in furthering the ideals of the R.S.C.M. are always especially anxious to be of use to the small and often remote country parishes. So often, however, I am confronted by remarks such as "Our choir is so bad—it would be a waste of your time to come and visit us". These are the choirs one especially wishes to visit and help if only because such remarks indicate a deep-seated fallacy which believes that a country choir must of necessity be bad and that little or nothing can be done by anyone to help.

In becoming affiliated to the R.S.C.M. a parish joins more than 8,000 others from all over the world. This vast community embraces not only the whole of the Anglican Communion but has now extended its work to include Free Church and Roman Catholic choirs.

YOUR CATHEDRAL

Ideally, all parish church organists should feel able to consult their Cathedral organist when advice is needed. It is therefore sad that some of the Cathedral organists (but by no means all) are stand-offish and view their amateur brother organists with indifference or even hostility, reluctantly approaching church music in the Diocese as a burdensome chore which has perforce to be lived with if one cannot entirely dispose of the necessity of having to deal with it.

On the other side it must be said that most Dioceses are blessed with one or two parish church organists who are difficult crosses to bear. We all suffer from those talkative people who if they get the chance—will habitually inhabit a cathedral organ loft to the exclusion of anyone else who may want to be there.

In these enlightened days negative attitudes coming from cathedral organists only serve to engender even further the Barchester-like image of many of our cathedral churches. As the Bishop is Father in God for the *pastoral* needs of his Diocese, so should a cathedral organist make part of his vocation the responsibility for the *musical* needs of the Diocese he serves. Some cathedral organists seem unaware of the existence of their Diocese or, for that matter, of anything outside the sleepy confines of the Close.

It ought however, in all fairness, to be said that at the present time more Cathedral organists than ever before are devoting much of their energy to work in the Diocese, though these are usually of the younger generation and more often than not those of the Parish Church Cathedrals who are anyhow much nearer the parishes.

Being more than aware of the chinks in my personal armour, I would never presume to cite myself as an example of what a cathedral organist's task should be, as related to the 20th century. I do however start with the advantage of thoroughly enjoying visits to choirs in my Diocese. The more I do this and the more contacts I make with clergy and laity alike and in trying to help and encourage those less fortunate than myself, the more I see it paying dividends. When annual festivals come round I see repeated evidence of improving standards, even if it is only in such simple things as said or sung Amens.

I am convinced that it is the friendly contact which counts, together with trying to understand the especial needs and problems of organists in country areas. It is after all the sort of encouragement, and perhaps inspiration, which only a Cathedral organist or someone in a similar position can give. This demands one being constantly out and about the Diocese; moreover, it snowballs—amazingly quickly—into a two-way traffic whereby organists and choirs come in to their Cathedral and feel they are part of it just as the mother Church is a part of them. Many Cathedral organists thus lead two entirely opposed lives, each adding valuable experience to the other.

My advice then is to take every opportunity of going to your Cathedral and of hearing the choir. Take your own choir and let them observe every aspect of the cathedral's standard and notice how such things ranging from psalm singing to said Amens and processing should be done. Good processing will usually be reflected in the singing, and *vice versa,* because the discipline of the one will be brought to bear on the discipline of the other. It matters not that the music they sing may be technically difficult by comparison with your own output; what does matter is that everything a Cathedral choir does should be an inspiring example for all the choirs of the Diocese to copy. This is a responsibility which some cathedral choirs discharge better than others. If you go to a cathedral and see the choir processing or kneeling untidily, go back to your own parish resolved to make your own processing the better because of it. It can work both ways.

In the end what matters is the sense of doing all things well and nothing, however humble or exalted, is worthy of less than the best in the worship of the Church. It is a sad reflection on the slovenly attitudes which often prevail over much of the religious activity in this country that time and again it could be very much better. It is the clergy who are frequently the weak link in this matter and do little or nothing towards improvement.

ADVANTAGES TO BE GAINED FROM TAKING PART IN FESTIVALS

Most of the activity of this nature is arranged either by the Diocesan Choral Association, if there is one, or by the R.S.C.M.

In the Exeter Diocese, as far as the former is concerned, the annual Festival which takes place in the Cathedral in June is prefaced by two preliminary events. One Saturday in the previous March the Cathedral Choir sing, in place of the normal Evensong, the music chosen for the ensuing Festival. Each year we find that more and more organists and choir members (sometimes complete choirs) come to hear the music and to get some idea of how it sounds. This has proved to be an invaluable aid to their own preparation of the music.

After the service I meet organists and discuss with them any points or queries which may have arisen and which need clarifying. Then, for some four or five weeks immediately prior to the Festival itself, I am out in the Diocese nearly every evening taking regional rehearsals. By this time the choirs should know the notes, (this is not always so), and I give them indications of speeds, of how I am going to conduct certain passages and what generally I intend to do when it comes to the Festival. As the average parish church choir seldom has to watch a conductor, I have to impress on choir members the need for this if the Festival is going to be anything of a musical success. Having been at pains to stress this point for some years, the choirs are now much more confident and do watch me (except for those few members who would never watch any conductor).

The choirs have seen for themselves the fruits of this in that we have now established a confident tradition that more than a thousand singers can keep together in a great Cathedral—provided they watch the beat. At the end of it all the chances are that choirs will go back to their parishes not only having enjoyed themselves but having learned something into the bargain as well. One hopes they will be spurred on to greater efforts by the experience of having formed an integral part of a great choir, an experience which for us all is a most memorable one. For the person who in his parish church choir happens to be the solitary tenor week by week, there is a great thrill in joining forces with a hundred other tenors!

Very often, smaller Deanery festivals are arranged and these provide an added measure of experience and proficiency either as a preliminary, or as a follow-up, to the main festival. One obstacle to progress in the Exeter Diocese—and probably in others—results from clergy who fail to pass on to their organist the circular containing details of the festival.

The R.S.C.M. Festivals at Exeter as in most other Dioceses, are carefully graded so as to be of help to all types of choir. Two of our most fruitful ventures have been the Evensong sung by Village and Small Parish Church choirs and the Hymn Singing Festivals. In the former we choose very simple music including canticles to chants and an easy anthem. This festival has increased in popularity year by year and, with the overall objective of singing the music really well, standard is an all-important incentive.

The Hymn Singing Festivals are planned to help both choirs and congregations in equal proportion. Here we always aim to introduce one or two new hymns, be it words or tune, or both. These may be in the accepted style though modern in outlook and may range from the music of Malcolm Williamson to Sydney Carter's *The Lord of the Dance.*

As choral festivals provide obvious opportunities for learning new music, especially hymn tunes, care must be exercised in the minds of the committee who decide on what is to be sung each year.

The one basic necessity of any choral festival is that choirs must necessarily know their notes before the day. This would seem to be an obvious start to the proceedings but experience points to frequent evidence of inadequate preparation which reflects the lack of conscience in some of the choirs taking part. Some choirmasters are versatile in thinking up excuses—some of them valid maybe—for having failed to learn the notes in good time. The fact remains that any choir less than note perfect is only a hindrance and annoyance to those who have gone to the trouble of learning the music.

When choirs are note-perfect the conductor is able to spend the rehearsal time moulding the music into a coherent whole which, in its turn, will serve as a model for all. This, after all, is the function of any conductor. Far too many church choirs get little further than mere notes and unfortunately seem to think that this alone will suffice.

If, as the result of a Choral Festival, every choir returns to its own parish with only one point of technique or performance better than before, then something has been achieved—and improved.

Festivals ought also to be a source of great pleasure to those taking part especially when it happens to be in the magnificent surroundings of a vast cathedral. On the lighter side there is the business of meeting other choirs socially, if only to eat sandwiches and discuss the respective merits—or otherwise—of vicars and organists!

Finally, an important point to remember. The morale of a choir is strengthened by hearing another choir whose standard of singing happens to be *lower* than theirs. While this is a natural reaction, it is very good for a choir to rub shoulders with a choir whose standard of performance is *higher* than its own. This is the sort of thing which happens at a choral festival and discerning choirs, together with their organists, will judge for themselves why this is so and, one hopes, be the wiser for the experience.

IMPROVING STANDARDS BY HELPING OURSELVES

1. As an organist, always practise even the most simple things. You teach (or ruin) your choir by example, often without being aware of it.

2. Always have a new voluntary on the stocks.

3. Raise your sights high and never be complacent. As was said earlier, most of us are capable of much higher standards than we care to credit ourselves with.

4. Never, either through pride or fear, fight shy of being told what is wrong. None of us relishes criticism, but we ought never to resent it when it is given in the right spirit and is constructive. If, as is likely, this criticism comes from someone in the pews, it is worth remembering that the musical effect there is probably quite different from where the organist and choir are situated. It is therefore quite conceivable that the criticism is valid.

One of the hazards of church work is that most of us are subject to our self-appointed "advisers", ever ready to let us have their unasked-for opinions. But we can always turn our deaf ear to them and our good ear to those who will just as gladly offer reasoned and sensible advice.

5. Never develop an inferiority complex; it is just as dangerous as a superiority one and just as damaging to those one comes into contact with. In a word, be confident of the ability which the good God has given you. Our talents mercifully are not equal.

6. It is useful to remember that the older we get the more we can learn. Once we stop learning, especially if we think we know enough already, the worst rot of all swiftly sets in.

7. Having asked for advice from a responsible person—take it. Many don't especially if it is unpalatable.

9 Clergy versus Organists
(with some incidentals)

In my opinion, parsons are very like other men, and neither the better nor the worse for wearing a black gown.
Philip Dormer Stanhope, Earl of Chesterfield (1694–1773)

As the French say, there are three sexes—men, women and clergymen.
Sydney Smith (1771–1845)

THE IDEAL PARTNERSHIP

I recently read an article by Martin Thornton on *Music and Ascetical Theology*. It began:

> There is an old tradition which sees the relation between Organist and Vicar as roughly that between cat and dog: by domestication they manage to exist together without physical violence while remaining natural enemies at heart. Times have happily changed and the idea of a creative interplay between music and liturgy is now taken for granted.

These are strong words. From my own experience I would say that times have *to a considerable extent* changed. All too frequently, however, a vicar will come to see me and proceed to complain about his organist. The chances are that he will be followed up (at a respectable distance of time) by the organist who in his turn complains about his vicar.

On reflection, these instances are often not without their touch of humour though there is much more to it than that. Most of the causes for complaint, though perhaps to some extent justified, are usually small ones which conflicting temperaments have magnified out of all proportion and which, in the first instance, should never have been the cause for strained relationships. The final indignation—at any rate for me personally—is, that having come to ask my advice, neither party generally heeds it in the slightest degree.

One is forced to the conclusion that there is something in the make-up of clergy and organists which on occasion impels them to behave both irresponsibly and irrationally.

Obvious to all are the repercussions of two apparently responsible adults, both in prominent parochial positions, being unable to see eye to eye. Much harm can be done to the cause of the Church by the inevitable tongue wagging which accompanies such incidents and which gives the man in the street plenty of incentive to hold forth on his favourite hobby horse of "the Church putting its own house in order . . ." etc. It usually transpires that neither party is entirely at fault nor entirely blameless. Pride enters very much into it and because of this both sides are fearful for their status and of their particular field of activity being encroached upon.

What a vicar expects of his organist, and *vice versa,* is virtually impossible to define in so many words as often where good relationships exist, they have been built on differing factors.

What one can say, and say positively, is that the relationship must ideally be a dual function in which each sees the other's point of view. Each must be aware of the other's specialised knowledge in his particular field of activity, however small or even inadequate though that knowledge may be. It must also be remembered that in this special relationship the vicar is a professional and the organist, in most instances, an amateur. This can contribute in no small measure towards "organist *versus* vicar" strife.

As both sides can be "prickly", the utmost forbearance—virtues not always to be found in church circles—must be exercised. It is at this vulnerable level that relationships tend to break down. A high-handed approach from either party, in which things are done and decisions taken without consultation, will often precipitate matters. The motives for such actions are perhaps hard to understand, unless at the root of it all there is a sense of guilt or of being unnecessarily fearful of one's status.

While much of this section of the book deals with problems which in fact do exist, together with ways and means of solving them, it must be said that there are many parishes (and cathedrals, for that matter) where clergy and musicians make it their business to see eye to eye and work happily together as a team to further the work of God's kingdom.

WHO CHOOSES THE HYMNS?

On this issue the blood so often rises! The parson, as the person at the top, obviously has the right to decide on the hymns. (Legally he has the right to do almost anything). Ideally, the organist ought to be consulted, not only in suggestions about tunes but because two heads are often better than one. One party can, and ought, to complement the other.

Should the parson choose the hymns, he must choose them well in advance otherwise he must not be surprised if choir and organist perform them badly. The tunes must also be decided on in good time. Such deplorable instances as that of correcting the organist, publicly at a service, after he has proceeded to play over a different tune, are not unknown. This sort of thing only serves to perpetuate the public image of the Church as an organisation thoroughly amateurish and disorganised, which in such cases is precisely what it is.

While the parson may have every reason to wish for a particular hymn at any one time, the choice of hymns could be very much more varied in most churches. Favourite hymns are "done to death" while only a small percentage of the contents of any one hymnbook are used. Another point to be borne in mind when choosing hymns is to avoid during the course of any one service, two or even three consecutive hymns in the same metre or time.

THE PARSON'S RESPONSIBILITY AND HIS POINT OF VIEW

The parson is ultimately responsible for everything which takes place in his church. In musical matters, as with other branches of parish activity, he frequently delegates this responsibility. Nevertheless the final word is his and his alone.

His musical concern should always be for the congregation's *rightful* part in the services—no more and no less. He comes up against his first obstacle with the organist who, in some instances, considers music to be more important than anything else which happens in church. Worship, especially in the Parish Communion, implies "togetherness", with *all* playing their respective parts, i.e. clergy, servers (if there are any), choir and laity.

One of the difficult problems facing the clergy today is that of the "new look" which is rapidly emerging and which in time may well assume the proportions of a second Reformation (if it is not already doing this). The experimental services now being tried out, notably the Series Two Communion Service, demand much care in presentation. No parish priest can, with any conscience, afford to ignore the implications of this. The Church's innate sense of conservatism can well prove a stumbling-block to the introduction of these new services, for some of the clergy, as well as choirs and congregations, are deeply rooted in the old ways and are loath to alter.

Music plays such an important role in Series Two that an added reluctance by organists and choir members to come to terms with far-reaching changes, many of which are necessary and justified in this day and age, can hinder the witness of the Church and retard any efforts being made in this direction by the clergy.

An organist often fails to appreciate the considerable degree to which the spirit of worship can be influenced by his playing. An organist who rightly devotes his energies to the music of the services sometimes fails to perceive, in the wider sense, the overall picture and the basic objective of corporate worship. Others consciously fight shy of this, conveniently brushing it aside with "my concern is the music". The organist's concern is Worship, of which music is but a part.

The parson, whose pastoral charge is to deal with people can often, through his wide experience of humanity at large, see the chinks in the organist's armour. But if he is to get anywhere and make any real progress in his already difficult task, he must needs approach the subject tactfully, especially if his organist is by nature suspicious or even hostile.

Salary

One important responsibility of the clergy is to see that the organist is given adequate and realistic remuneration for what he does. To say that many organists are imposed upon in this direction is considerably to understate the case, for the business of devoting an evening or two each week to choir practice and to play for Sunday services, all for around £50 a year, is more than a labour of love. But for the fact that the average organist is a dedicated person—(he has to be at such rates of pay)—it would be even more difficult than it is at the present time to find organists.

The parish will get a better return from a financially contented organist. The often-quoted statement "The labourer is worthy of his hire" is not without some element of truth.

THE PARSON'S VIEW ON THE RELEVANCE OF MUSIC IN WORSHIP

Some of the clergy have strong views on this subject. Some feel that, good or indifferent though it may be, it serves no useful purpose—a point of view which is hard to justify. If any parson is thinking along these lines he should proceed to sack both organist and choir and work out his own musicless salvation as best he can.

The clergy who believe in the value of music as an important ingredient of worship are mercifully very much in the majority and, because of this, give their musicians every support and help though a few are sometimes guilty both of dishonesty and anything but fair dealing. Evidence of some very shoddy treatment of organists comes to my knowledge from time to time; it is unfortunate that those responsible are not likely to read this book.

Even if a parson is unmusical he ought, from time to time, to put in an appearance at choir practices. This showing of interest and appreciation for those who are making the effort to give up time to serve the Church, never fails to pay dividends. While this evidences some sign of understanding human relationships, it is very different from the tactless verbal intrusions made upon a choir rehearsal by some of the clergy.

A wise parson will take his organist into his confidence and will explain what he wants—and why. The last thing he will do is to treat his organist as a hired underling—which he isn't.

No parish priest can afford to neglect the musical aspect of worship. Most members of congregations are much more aware of musical values today than they might have been twenty years ago. Today there is so much opportunity for hearing good music well performed that, if our church music is offensive—as it sometimes is—it acts as a deterrent and people will stay away from church because of it. This is a known fact. The parson cannot wash his hands of it and say "the music is the organist's job".

THE ORGANIST'S POINT OF VIEW

Whatever happens, the organist will zealously guard the music. It is, after all, his own kingdom and music has every right to be an important factor, contributing to the wholeness of Christian worship.

He may, as we said earlier, complain about his salary, often with due cause. There are clergy who only too readily take more than fair advantage of the ideal of "serving the Church". This expression becomes the panacea for all ills and is often used to make the unfortunate organist feel uncomfortable and even embarrassed. The clergy tend to labour the point, though often quite unjustifiably, simply because they themselves are continually being encroached upon and taken for granted. The lot of a country parson today is not necessarily a happy one nor is his status symbol in that parish what it once was while the chances are that he may be saddled, into the bargain, with the problems of running a large and perhaps dreary vicarage.

Nevertheless, a P.C.C., if they want music, must not only be prepared to pay a reasonable salary to the organist and choirmaster, but also provide the necessary music if they expect the set-up to function in a businesslike way. They must also be prepared, if necessary, to robe the choir (although there is nothing against having an unrobed choir). The P.C.C. must agree to do these things ungrudgingly. It is not generally known that there is an official scale of salaries for organists in every type of church. Called the Ashfield Scale, it is obtainable from the Royal College of Organists.

Some organists are biased over matters of churchmanship, others merely uninterested. Nevertheless, the organist who says "I don't like the Mass" should not become organist of a church where the churchmanship is of that kind. Similarly, a convinced high churchman will never be happy playing Mattins Sunday by Sunday in an evangelical church. Therefore never accept an appointment where the brand of churchmanship is diametrically opposed to your own.

The lack of security of tenure can often prove the most explosive aspect of an organist's work. Most clergy and organists behave with irreproachable scruple, but the fact nevertheless remains that an organist can be summarily dismissed by the Incumbent and with no appeal allowable to the Bishop. A system such as this can lead to much unfair and unwarranted treatment (though organists have been known to drive vicars to distraction). When such a situation arises it often escalates with dire results which can split a parish down the middle. Quite apart from this, there is the untold harm caused by the more popular elements of the Press being only too ready to leap in for the kill. Anything negative which can blacken the image of the Church is fair sport to much of the Press. The involvement of the Press is such today that a priest celebrating fifty years of faithful ministry is of little or no news value compared with the lay reader who runs off with the vicar's wife.

Security of tenure is often imperilled through the lack of any written agreement made between the P.C.C. and the organist. In many cases we must be thankful that parson and organist trust each other and neither party feels the need to be bound by the strict letter of the law. This is perfectly all right until your vicar moves to another living and you find yourself saddled with a very different type of master.

Therefore, whatever the situation may be, a legal agreement ought always, from a business point of view, to be entered upon by *both* parties. In it, duties, salary, extra fees and holidays should all be clearly set out and understood by all parties concerned. The Royal College of Organists issue *A suggested Form of Agreement between the Incumbent and church authorities of a parish church and the Organist and Choirmaster, issued under the authority of the College.* This can be highly recommended as a basis for any P.C.C. *versus* organist partnership.

THE DANGERS OF THE ORGANIST CONCERNED ONLY WITH MUSIC AND NOT NECESSARILY WITH WORSHIP AS A WHOLE

It is, on all counts, highly desirable that an organist be a practising Christian and not merely a nominal member of the Church. Although his task is primarily that of playing the organ and training the choir, this should not exclude him from taking a fully active part, as a communicant, in the corporate life of his church and parish. This "cult" of being a person apart denies him the opportunity not only of meeting people but of making the contacts which will obviously help in his recruiting of new choir members, for it is never easy in these days to find people willing to be regularly committed. Many clergy say of their organist "Oh, we never see him, other than playing the organ on Sundays" or "He keeps himself to himself".

The organist's sphere of influence lies of course much deeper than in merely training the choir musically. His teaching of young and old alike in such things as reverence, deportment and general behaviour (remember that a chancel choir is always visible to the congregation), will either be a help or a hindrance to worship. At its best it can provide something of great value to the effective life of the Church at large.

All this can only be attained by example. Again and again one reverts to the Church's infinite capacity for encouraging slipshod attitudes which affect the organist no less than the clergy. The organist who knows how to behave decently and is constantly at pains to see that his choir does the same, will invariably add something of beauty and lasting value to the services. Choir discipline is both personal and corporate and is reflected in many ways. The good choirmaster will be at pains to make his choir know *why* these things are necessary but it is to our lasting shame that today discipline is in many quarters all but frowned on while "self expression' is regarded as the open sesame to most things. The organist who places small value on such necessities as discipline, or fails in putting it into practice, is considerably restricting his potential achievement.

THE PARSON'S PART IN THE SERVICES

Should he be expected to be musical?

The conduct of the services, as far as the parson is concerned, is something which should be continually claiming his attention. Good presentation and even a good sense of theatre, both in said and sung parts, are necessary if the services are to have any lasting impact on the congregation.

Intoning

> This particularly rapid, unintelligible patter
> Isn't generally heard, and if it is it doesn't matter.
>
> *W. S. Gilbert:* RUDDIGORE

What of the parson who cannot sing in tune? Many of the clergy are well aware that it is notoriously difficult to intone. Even the most experienced professional singers find it hard to keep accurately on one note for any length of time. While the clergy may be aware of their deficiencies in this respect, few are prepared to practise, either with the choir or on their own. The answer to the plea "I am tone deaf" is "Then let someone else do it". There is no reason why a member of the choir should not sing the priest's part in the responses and also intone the collects. If the parson's singing voice leaves much to be desired, this procedure is preferable and certainly more edifying for all concerned. In any event, the parson's real job is to be a good parish priest, the ability to sing being a sideline. The simple truth is that the good God did not give singing voices to all of us, a fact we must accept and act on accordingly.

Plunket Greene, in his book *Interpretation in Song* (Macmillan, 1921), has devoted an informed and extremely witty chapter to "The clergy and intoning". It is well worth reading.

Said parts

It is here that so many inexcusable parsonic habits creep in. The unnatural voice adopted by some clergy once they are in church is entirely indefensible on any grounds; it only serves to give the Church's critics—and mimics—plenty of ammunition.

We hear much today on the subject of the "archaic" language of the Liturgy. While one can point to many obscure phrases and what, to the 20th century ears, are strange turns of grammar, the beauty of the prose contained in the Book of Common Prayer can never, in its own right, be in doubt even if not everyone can readily appreciate what it all means. Cranmer's language, which has stood the test of centuries, is an expression of our literary heritage. One wonders if, in fact, it is questioned more or understood less today than it has been all the way down the years.

Be it archaic and obscure in its language, be it Series Two or be it Cecil Day Lewis's version of the Canticles, it is all but criminal that far too frequently what is recited publicly in church can be made to sound so dull and utterly meaningless. The beauty of any Liturgy needs, for its interpretation, a strong sense of drama and of timing if it is to get across and transmit to the listener a message which is something more than mere words.

Much of the problem surely lies in the repetitive nature of our services which frequently leads to parrot-fashion participation by clergy and laity alike. The basic similarity of Mattins and Evensong does not help matters. We become lazy and even lethargic, mumbling away each Sunday with our heads buried in our hands and our thoughts frequently anywhere but on what should be occupying our attention. The clergy, who should be the very people to hold our attention and fire us with some "revelation of that divine beauty" are, in so many instances, guilty of rushing through the services as if speed alone were the one necessary means to salvation.

In an age when impeccable public speaking is the order of the day in certain (though by no means all) sections of radio, television and the theatre, it is not surprising that many discerning people stay away from church because they will not put up with the way in which the clergy conduct the services. It may well be that those who stay away from church for these reasons do so for wrong motives, but anyone attending a church service has the right to hear it read in an intelligible way. Church acoustics can be notoriously difficult for the listener and this, apart from any other considerations, places an especial onus on the clergy.

In my visits around the Exeter Diocese (which is probably neither better nor worse in these matters than any other) I am constantly obliged to listen to clergy who apparently have little notion of how to communicate what they have to say with any convincing impact. They fail in such things as:

1. Projecting their voices, as would an actor, to the farthest corners of the church—and not necessarily boomingly loud.

2. Rushing. It is a well known fact (not always put into practice) that public speaking in a building of any size requires a speaker to talk more deliberately than he would in an informal conversation. This includes giving due time for short words such as "and", "the" and "for" etc.

3. The habit of gabbling and a breathless pursuit of prayer! We have all, at one time or another, been subjected to the parson who starts the next prayer before choir and congregation have had time to say "Amen" to the previous one. It sometimes works the other way as well when "keen" members of the congregation come in with "And with thy spirit" before the parson has finished "The Lord be with you". Speaking generally and allowing for exceptions, it can very often be summed up by saying "The higher the churchmanship, the quicker the gabbling".

4. An apparently total unawareness of the rhythm of the words or for the need to space them out.

5. Over-announcing of hymns. As most churches have hymn boards why announce them at all? Pedantic preambles such as "And now shall we sing hymn number three hundred and sixty-five? Praise, my soul, the king of heaven. The three hundred and sixty-fifth hymn" assumes that the congregation cannot see and has no intelligence.

6. Most important of all, as previously mentioned, the "clerical delivery". It is an unmitigated stupidity which does credit to no one and only serves even further to present the church as an archaic, and slightly comic, institution out of touch with the world of today.

The clergy and the R.S.C.M.

While many clergy consult the R.S.C.M. over such things as the choice of music, the appointment of organists and the re-building of organs, it is not always realised that *practical* help is available for the clergy themselves. The R.S.C.M. is concerned not merely with choirs but with all who serve the Church and its music.

In this respect, courses for ordinands may also be attended by clergy who want to take a refresher course in the conduct of public worship. The R.S.C.M. also publishes *Praises with Understanding,* a very useful book which contains a wealth of information for clergy anxious to take their services in the best possible way. This "practical handbook for ordinands and clergy", by the Reverend Horace Spence, a former Clerical Commissioner of the R.S.C.M., is the outcome of forty years of ministry in town and country.

SUMMARY

Some of the clergy need to be reminded that whatever the limitations, annoying habits or other faults an organist may have, he is, within the limits of his capabilities and with the resources at his command, endeavouring to maintain some standard in what may well be none too rewarding a task. Above all else he needs encouragement and the parson is the key person to give this. Many remote country organists who come into this category are disheartened when their clergy give them no encouragement and no support when things are especially difficult.

On the other side there are the organists who need to be reminded that one of the main functions of music in worship is to lead, for worship implies doing things *together* as a community. The organist who, with a highly inflated opinion of himself and his works, believes that music alone matters, is on the wrong wavelength and must expect—sooner or later—to be confronted with his own inevitable downfall.

Tact, partnership and unselfishly seeing the other point of view are essential ingredients in the parson *versus* organist relationship. In the end it is a question of mutual trust for, if the Church is to flourish, the business of all parties learning to live together in small communities (not the easiest proposition at any time), is going to be one of the top priorities.

10 Recruiting choir members and organists

WHY ARE MANY CHURCH CHOIRS SO DEPLETED TODAY?

A number of factors are responsible for the sorry state of church music which prevails at the present time in many parishes.

1. As far as *town* parishes are concerned, the trend in recent years has been for the population to move out of the centre either into the country or into housing estates in the suburbs. Many major parish churches situated in the centre of cities and large towns have been hard hit, both congregationally and otherwise, through this shift of population. For those who have moved yet wish to remain loyal to their own parish church, considerable transport problems may arise, especially for those not yet old enough to drive a car. This can affect matters to such an extent that eventually some will decide either to go to a church near at hand—or more probably give up altogether.

2. In *country* parishes, where life tends to remain more static, the problems today are probably little different from what they always were. The harvest still has to be brought in and the cows milked.

In my experience, some of the best singing I hear often comes, surprisingly enough, from village choirs. In the hands of a choir-master who really knows his (or her) job, a remarkably high standard of singing is produced and maintained. In these all too rare instances hard work, boundless drive and a compelling personality—plus a little genius—all seem to combine to bring this about.

3. *The new Society.* Choirs are but one of the many organisations affected by this. As a nation, the vast majority of the population today are not only non-churchgoers but also non-Christians. Young children coming from such a background rarely find any parental encouragement if, and when, they join a church choir.

The rapidly emerging pattern of a five-day week, plus the fact that so many households now possess a car, means that entire families go away for the weekend or spend their Sundays away from home. From this, in a roundabout way, we see something of the reasons for the growth of the Parish Communion for, having done your duty and been to church, the rest of the day is your own to spend as and how you wish. While this works admirably in those parishes where this is the pattern of events, it also partly explains perhaps why in other parishes, Mattins at 11 o'clock and Evensong at 6.30 have less drawing power.

4. *The distractions of today and how they affect the Church.* The world around us, as we know only too well, provides much to distract most of us. Everything from television to bingo and drugs is readily at hand to divert us from our commitments, especially if we happen to be just that bit weak willed. Because of this, the Church tends to fare badly, especially when many of these distractions prove more interesting than going to church.

The archaic image, together with the language and customs which the Church employs, genuinely embarrasses many young people and deters them from becoming would-be choristers. To the committed Christian this is perhaps an impertinent assumption but to the uncommitted outsider it is a very real deterrent, for they see the Church as something thoroughly alien and living out a shaky existence in an unreal atmosphere, (which is often a very fair assessment of the facts).

If the services in many of our churches were less dreary and stereotyped, the problem of recruiting organists and choristers might, in its turn, be less formidable. The Church has some reputation—not without an element of truth—for attracting oddities and cranks, in or out of Holy Orders. While this may be so, if the Church as a whole were to be more readily identified with the people and less "ecclesiastically" inward-looking, its appeal to the man in the street might be more obvious. We all know of the "live" parishes and it is generally easy to see the reason why.

5. *Loyalty—its diminishing role.* One of the most cancerous evils eating into the roots of society today is that of complacency, a regard only for one's self and, in many instances, coming and going as one wishes regardless of a sense of loyalty. One is constantly having to make people aware of the fact that in joining any organisation, especially a voluntary one, they conscientiously support it as an active member of the team. Most choirmasters, at one time or another, have good cause to complain of the ill effects resulting from the increasing abandonment of loyalty, and this we are witnessing in most walks of our national life. Moreover, the courtesy of an apology for non-attendance, in advance or otherwise, seems more often than not to be a thing of the past.

Another tiresome cross which any choirmaster has to bear is the choir member (usually aged around sixty) who unfailingly absents himself from choir practice on the grounds that "I've been in the choir for over forty years and I know it all". Invariably he will be the type of singer so set in his habits—and often bad ones—that he is more in need of rehearsal than many of his younger and more enlightened colleagues. The singer who obstinately persists in this policy of no rehearsal, and is allowed to get away with it, is a heavy liability to his fellow singers when he takes his place in the stalls on a Sunday. It is perhaps only fair to say that this attitude is sometimes the result of having to bear for years with intolerably dull and uninspired practices; if this is so, the choirmaster ought to take stock and rethink his own attitudes and methods.

The necessity for regular attendance at rehearsals must constantly be stressed as something of the utmost importance if a choir is going to strive for and—most difficult of all—maintain a standard. The example which the choirmaster sets is invaluable if it is impeccable. If he himself gives a high priority to regular choir practices, the chances are that the choir might do the same.

6. *Bad influences and their effects*. There is always a nucleus of those who sing in church choirs who apparently have no yardstick by which to measure their standard of performance. Such people, often complacently lazy, see no urgent need to improve their standards and are probably quite unaware of the deplorable sounds they may be producing. Any suggestion of the need for improvement is immediately resented (behind your back, of course) or dismissed as impertinent criticism. It is certain that anyone with any real feeling for the team spirit of choral singing will not stay the course for long in a choir where such conditions are allowed to prevail.

It is to the shame of the clergy that they often fight shy of backing up their organist in dealing with offenders. In such matters, the decisive backing of the Vicar would give the choirmaster the support and authority he needs when confronted with this type of situation. In most instances, the Vicar will take no positive action; in trying to placate all parties, his dove of peace flutters with little effect and his final word is usually to the effect that to depose the offender would be "un-Christian". In the end, the continued presence of such a person in the choir is more likely to harm the cause of religion than to further it. Similarly, most choirs are saddled with one particular member who delights in being awkward; no sooner has he departed from the scene than another takes his place as the unofficial "shop steward".

Organists who have little notion of how to accompany are equally effective at helping to drive musical people out of the choir. Many of the turgid, insensitive and overpowering sounds which result from this merely encourage choir and congregation alike either to give up in despair against the unequal odds or transfer to another church (where things may be no better).

Rhythm and vitality might be considered by not a few organists as a tolerable substitute for a mere volume of sound.

The final danger is the parson who sees no need for a choir at all. Spurred on by the belief that the congregation will never sing well while a choir exists, he disbands at one stroke a choir which has perhaps done very creditable and loyal service for many years. It is also conceivable that the tradition thus built up has done something to enhance the worship, though this will not be apparent to the Vicar. A choir can be swiftly and effectively disbanded overnight but when a new Vicar with other ideas comes on the scene he will find it may take many years to build up the choral tradition once again.

RECRUITING ORGANISTS

While parishes often have to make do without a choir, a church without an organist finds itself severely restricted. As a last resort, someone who is not really an organist may volunteer to play for services and perhaps take choir practices solely because there is no one else available. As a result, the volunteer finds his own level, often without preconceived notions; this can be all to the good and the resulting achievement the more praiseworthy.

Even so, the scarcity of organists is becoming more and more acute, nor is it likely to alter much in the foreseeable future. Many an organist needs to be a truly dedicated person, with something of a saint in him, to allow himself to be tied Sunday by Sunday, often with little hope of finding a deputy when he wants to go on holiday. The chances are that he will be disheartened by the sounds coming from the choir who may, or may not, be doing their best; he may also be expected to play an instrument which, although once splendid, is now all but falling apart through years of neglect. He may be dispirited, though he will not necessarily show it publicly, by the lack of interest or by the complete indifference which some clergy so liberally display towards their organist. The financial reward, when he has paid his Income Tax and his petrol, makes his work little more than a labour of love.

With the dice so heavily loaded in many parishes up and down the land, is it surprising that relatively few people today seriously consider the prospect of becoming parish church organists?

The subject of salary was mentioned in the previous chapter. The inadequacy of what in many cases is offered is all but an insult to an intelligent person and only serves to provide a yet further deterrent to would-be organists. The argument sometimes put forward by clergy and P.C.C.'s is that an organist, being an amateur, should expect little more than an honorarium to cover expenses; he should "serve the Church for the love of it". This may be a worthy ideal but an organist will often work far better, and less grudgingly, when the miserable pittance which may have been his lot for many a long year becomes more realistically linked with the continually rising cost of petrol. It is, however, encouraging to see some increase in the average level of salaries being offered when posts are advertised, even though the increase may have been prompted by the church authorities realising only too well that they are otherwise unlikely to attract a suitable candidate.

Under some of the current conditions it is hardly surprising that fewer and fewer organists, especially those of the younger generation, are prepared to be committed to what is virtually sweated labour. The consequences can be seen in many promising musicians being lost to the Church.
(See "Some Personal Comments" by Dr. Gerald H. Knight. (*English Church Music 1968,* published by the Royal School of Church Music).

Having dealt, to some extent, with the picture as it applies in certain parishes today, what of the future? In the light of the foregoing remarks it is essential that young, promising and not so promising organists be helped and encouraged. The aims of the Somerset Organist Training Scheme are directed towards improving "the supply of organists for churches and chapels of all denominations in both town and village". Administered through the Evening Institutes, the scheme is worked on a group principle whereby a minimum of five students, over the age of fifteen, are given tuition in "the basic principles of organ playing in all its aspects to the beginner, and to improve the standards of existing players who already have Organists' appointments".

This admirable scheme is one which other counties might usefully adopt; in any event, P.C.C.'s might well consider paying for a series of lessons for a promising young organist in the parish; they could also arrange for him to attend one of the R.S.C.M. courses for organists and choirmasters. By showing a lively interest in such ways, more young men and women will perhaps be encouraged to become church organists. It will be money well spent.

While no opportunity in this respect should be lost, the persons concerned should themselves make every effort to improve their talents by visiting their cathedral whenever this is possible. Much can be learned from regularly sitting in a cathedral organ loft. By watching and hearing the organist accompany, especially the psalms, one assimilates the meaning of organ "colour" and of how to exploit the available resources to the best advantage. As for many others, my own experience, as a pupil of Sir Edward Bairstow at York Minster, was a tremendously inspiring help and example.

A country organist must ensure, in every way possible, that he is in touch with all that is happening in the world of church music. He must always *want* to broaden his vision; that means treading new and often exciting paths rather than following the somewhat restricted and often introspective ways of church music, otherwise this in itself can be too self-sufficient and narrow up the field of vision. Church music is a small if relatively important part of our musical heritage.

WAYS AND MEANS OF FINDING CHOIR MEMBERS—AND KEEPING THEM

Boys (or girls). Local schools ought to be the obvious places to start any recruiting. The first step is for the choirmaster to win the Head Master on to his side, if this is needed. Once this is done, his active support and interest can be of immense help all the way along the line. The Vicar can—and ought—to be equally useful, both because of his position and through his visiting in the parish. He is likely to be in touch with most newcomers to the parish and will thus know of choir members who have moved from other choirs or of those who might like to become choristers.

From time to time most parishes are forced to resort to a "drive" for recruiting choristers. For the purpose of setting out the relevant facts, an informative leaflet such as that issued by the Bradford Diocesan Committee of the R.S.C.M. is an admirably-worded handout and could well serve as a general model. These and other means, if one is persistent enough, can sometimes be fruitful but all too often after a few weeks, many of the newcomers may have disappeared, never to be seen in church again. While the organist may wring his hands in despair and bemoan his bad luck, experience shows that he seldom thinks of following up their disappearance or finding out the reasons for it. Making contact with the parents can often help to smoothe over any difficulties (which in the event are often trivial) and which may have accounted for the disappearance of the newcomer. Getting to know the parents of one's choristers can also help to forge an invaluable link throughout a boy's singing career.

On the face of it, it may be asking too much to suggest that the choirmaster visits the parents *immediately* any boy or girl fails to put in an appearance in the choir. Doing this will inevitably demand much time and energy but a conscientious choirmaster must be prepared to do this sort of thing if he wants his choir to hang together. Such action may well be instrumental in winning over a first-rate chorister—and maybe the parents as well—all of whom might otherwise be lost to the Church.

The all too familiar blank spaces in the choir stalls resulting from members who, for one reason or another, move away from the district provide further problems for a choirmaster, for it nearly always seems to be the best type of singer who moves on to become someone else's gain. From organists I often hear the sad tale of how many good boys they have lost in the past months, but hardly ever the glad news of how many promising recruits they have gained. Perhaps some of it is the luck of the game, or localised, but the general impression would seem to indicate a disturbingly dangerous swing in the wrong direction. It might be useful to have in mind the directive to "go out into the highways and hedges and compel them to come in" (Luke 14:23).

Discipline, both in rehearsal and at services, is essential if any group of singers, young or old, is to work as a team. Ultimately, if you persist for long enough and explain the reason why, the toughest set of boys may learn to behave themselves in a decent fashion. They will respect you more for your insistence on this, for most people at heart prefer discipline and orderliness rather than the uncontrolled chaos which is allowed to persist in some choirs. The example set by the choirmaster in his own personal code of behaviour will very largely determine the measure of success or failure in this respect.

The R.S.C.M.'s Chorister Training Scheme can be a very useful aid in that choristers not only take on responsibility but also, visually and competitively, see their weekly progress on charts. Badges, together with chorister's handbooks and diaries, are other visible and tangible rewards which mean much to the average boy in terms of being fully committed. A really loyal and hard working chorister, with a sense of leadership, is one of the greatest assets any organist can wish for.

A choirmaster's interest in his boys ought not to be confined solely to their choir work. If he shows himself equally interested in their 'out of choir' activities, they will generally respond, and any efforts he makes in that direction will rarely misfire.

In the days when I was organist of Ripon Cathedral I found that most of my Saturdays were given over to a variety of pursuits involving the choristers. On our push bikes we explored much of the Vale of York. The main line from King's Cross to Edinburgh was not all that far away and more often than not we would spend some of our time train spotting. That, incidentally, was in the pre-Diesel era when engines were still worth looking at!

On other occasions we would play football or cricket. Although I was never much good at either and they knew this only too well, it helped us to get to know each other away from the practice room and I like to think these activities contributed towards any measure of success we were able to achieve when singing.

Most of these outings concluded, by North Country tradition, with a visit to the Fish and Chip shop or, if I was with the Lay Clerks, to the "local". The choir situation at Ripon in those days was a very difficult one, for we had to maintain five weekday Evensongs, as well as the Sunday services, with boys drawn from local day schools. In a market town of less than 10,000 people this was not always easy.

Not all of us have the gift—which is given only to a very few—of being the type of person who can not only muster and keep a large choir when other parishes all around seem to have such meagre resources, but can also mould his choir into a musically sensitive body of singers whose performance is second to none.

The successful choirmaster is one who inspires his singers to feel that being in a choir provides them with worthwhile enjoyment. He must understand something of liturgy, appreciating the beauty of words and communicating this to the choir, (this means the avoidance of such things as a clammy and sentimental approach to the *Nunc dimittis*). He must always be mindful of the implications of choristership and of his important task of training his boys in the service of God, much of it during the impressionable years of adolescence. The wise choirmaster will decide what measures he must take to help a boy once his voice has broken; it is not enough merely to say thank you and goodbye, for the average boy will not take easily to suddenly finding himself sitting in the pews as an individual, virtually unemployed and waiting for his voice to settle down before he is allowed to return to the choir.

Men. The problems here are of a different type and more difficult to deal with as adults are far less pliable than children. They are frequently "set" in their ways at a surprisingly early age and are therefore less able—or willing—to change. Whereas a good choirmaster can mould the voice of a "raw" boy at an early age, the fully-formed voice of the adult is a different proposition, as habits already formed are far less easy to break. With adults, business and family ties may well have caused your best tenor to be absent from the choir. For these and other reasons one expects a lesser degree of regularity in attendance from most adult singers.

The best all round choirman is often one who has been a boy chorister first. He remembers his training, is often proud of it, and applies its principles to his adult singing. Therefore, when a boy's voice breaks, do all you can to keep the croaking owner in the choir even though he may not be able to contribute much while his new voice is in the process of settling down. Many potential tenors and basses are lost to the Church because they are not retained in the service of the choir when their time as trebles comes to an end. Although they may be asked to rejoin the choir when their adult voices have settled down, experience repeatedly shows that the break away from regular routine often proves fatal. Quite apart from what was said earlier, other interests, worthy or otherwise, claim the attention of the impressionable adolescent, interests which may in the end take priority.

This losing of youth is sad for the choirmaster, as the training of a boy chorister ought to lead to fulfilment in the adult ranks of the choir. One likes to think that the discipline and training derived from impressionable years in a good choir will be of service in adult life. While the adolescent voice is settling down there is no harm in doing some singing provided it is not too loud, too high, too low or too protracted.

Whatever the capabilities of your men may be, at least train them to attempt to sing—and hold—a part. The habit in some choirs of habitually resorting to the tune an octave lower is more often than not an unmusical growl.

In recruiting men, be prepared with the help of your Vicar to seek out any newcomers to the parish who might be an asset to the choir. This again will cost time and effort but, in the end, is worth it. You will feel far from pleased if a neighbouring organist gets there before you and secures the services of someone who may be a first-rate singer.

Women and girls. It is a generally accepted fact that nowadays boy choristers are hard to find, though I am continually impressed by the proportion of boys' voices at most choral festivals, even if some of them do not appear to contribute very much! A boy's natural voice produced effortlessly and without strain is of course the ideal. At its best it causes American visitors to gasp with superlatives at a tradition which is so essentially English.

However, beggars are in no position to choose, and women choristers are increasingly supplanting boys in many parishes. Where women and girls are in the choir stalls, many parallel problems will arise, though their voices do not generally break!

Ideally, boys ought not to be mixed with women. To blend such different *timbres* is virtually impossible unless the women try to sing like boys. Teenage girls can do this admirably but to an outsize middle-aged woman the feat is both impossible and unthinkable. Where women and boys are together in the same choir, the boys are liable to take life too easily and allow the women to get on with most of the work.

Be it boys, women or men, the choirmaster must of necessity show interest in his singers, in their lives and in their families. The inevitable choir outing brings much happiness to the recipients and helps to increase the team spirit.

The members of the choir should, in their turn, be impressed by the privilege and honour of serving the Church in this particular way. It is only fair perhaps to say that most are, except those who saunter through life seemingly unimpressed by anybody or anything. A church choir is performing a unique and important task but must always be conscious of the need for doing *all* things really well.

A choir should cause the choirmaster much hard work. If at times they drive him to exasperation or if he experiences constant disappointment at their efforts, take heart, for all of us in our varying spheres of activity have the same experience from time to time. As mentioned earlier in this chapter choir members, young and old alike, have the infuriating habit of absenting themselves without notice, often on major occasions. This we apparently have to accept as part of the social pattern of life today but it is a sad reflection of the malaise which surrounds us. Nevertheless life has to go on and the choirmaster must perservere undaunted; he must do everything in his power to make practices so interesting and worthwhile that it becomes more of an attraction than the serial thriller being shown on television at the same time.

As a matter of priority, the choir must be impelled with enthusiasm and encouragement. Every choir needs both ingredients in large and repeated doses. The outlook for the future is not generally very reassuring. While less and less man hours of work per week become the accepted norm, with it there comes an inevitably diminishing sense of duty plus an increasing desire of "each for himself".

Nowadays, choirmasters often live considerable distances from their churches. This obviously makes for added difficulties which have to be surmounted as one of the occupational hazards of the job.

If you have no choir and have to start building one up from rock bottom, there is the unique and ready-made opportunity for you to mould a tradition. Start simply, persuading your choir and yourself, if necessary, of the virtues of unison singing. Most choirs need convincing that unison singing can be an artistic alternative to part-singing and that, whatever else unison may be, it is not something beneath a choir's dignity.

THE IMPORTANCE OF EXTRA INCENTIVES

For the choir there must, from time to time, be musical climaxes. These will vary according to the choir and the parish, but choral festivals, as mentioned earlier, can always be relied upon to provide a stimulus, except to those self-opinionated choirs who would benefit much from the help which such a festival provides but who find it beneath their dignity to take part. Such choirs can usually be relied upon to be so taken up with their own pride and misplaced sense of importance as to be oblivious to anything else.

To sing in new surroundings, often in the magnificence of your cathedral, and with different people around you, is something to look forward to and to remember afterwards. It is also a privilege.

The last word on the subject is for the clergy. Bearing in mind the shortage of organists, no parish priest ought to dismiss his organist unless he is both musically and personally irresponsible and, because of this, the worship of the parish is being jeopardised. He may well have irritating faults (so perhaps has the Vicar) but the chances are that he is doing the job to the best of his ability. If the Vicar does decide to dispense with his organist it may well be that he will find it very difficult to replace him, especially if it is a country parish. There is an old saying worth remembering—"The devil you know is better than the devil you don't know".

In the final count it can all be summed up very simply, for, it is no exaggeration to say that if a choir is really worth joining, it will seldom be short of recruits.

11 Some general observations

KEEPING THE ORGAN IN GOOD REPAIR

Bearing in mind that many church organs are very old, it is the more remarkable that they function as well as they do. This is in part due to the craftsmanship of the organ builders up and down the country who flourished in the latter half of the last century. Nearly all of them, or their successors, have by now been bought up by the larger firms but the quality of their work, together with the materials they used, is borne out by the degree of usefulness still to be found in their often untouched work.

For these reasons alone, it is important that organs are tuned, maintained and regulated by reputable firms. The work should be done at regular intervals in much the same way as one's car is serviced. This not only avoids any breakdown but helps towards getting the best out of the instrument.

As a policy, it is wise to remember that most organs ought to be stripped and cleaned every twenty years or so; in this respect it is a false economy to be cheeseparing. Quite apart from wear and tear and the needs for replacing any worn mechanism, most organs suffer from the amount of dirt which accumulates in them, especially in old churches.

If the time has come for a more extensive overhaul, the occasion should be used as an opportunity for improving the instrument, tonally and otherwise. Although the organist may well have his own ideas as to the nature and extent of the work needing to be done, a wise P.C.C. (who in the end will be responsible for finding the money), will do well to seek the advice of experts such as their Cathedral organist, the Diocesan Advisory Committee or the Organs Advisory Committee in London. As costs are continually rising, the longer the work is delayed the greater will be the probability that more extensive work will need doing. If, in place of an organ, a church possesses a harmonium, electronic organ or piano, the same applies. No instrument should be allowed to get into such a state of disrepair that the cost of renovation will in the end be almost beyond the resources of the church.

It is when faced with a financial *cul de sac* that an electronic instrument is sometimes considered as an attractive substitute for a pipe organ. It may be cheaper and it may look good in the illustrated catalogue (what doesn't?), but artistically it is very poor by comparison with the real thing and has nowhere near the life span of a pipe organ. Moreover, the next generation in the parish may well have good cause to bemoan the short-sighted policy which brought this about.

HINTS ON HAVING THE ORGAN OVERHAULED OR REBUILT

> You organists are like jaded cab-horses: always longing for another stop.
>
> *Sydney Smith* (1771–1845)

1. As previously mentioned, always ask the advice of the musical experts and, if a change in the position of the instrument is being contemplated, the architectural pundits.

2. On their recommendation, ask for estimates from two or three builders.

3. When coming to a decision, do not necessarily accept the lowest tender as a matter of course. Be guided in this by the expert and always remember that in the end you get only what you pay for.

4. If new stops are to be added, be certain they are really needed and are not being asked for merely because such-and-such a stop will be a cause for personal pride on the part of the organist.

There are far too many organs which are too big for the size of the church and, as most organists play far too loudly for most of the time, this aspect should be very carefully considered when drawing up a specification. Conversely, there are churches where the opposite is true and in which the organ is in fact too small for the building, or appears to be because the organist seldom uses the full range of available stops.

5. The fashion at the present time is to unclutter the chancels which were cluttered up by the ideals of the Oxford Movement. The usual move is to put the organ in a gallery (if there is one) at the West end of the church. While in many instances this is admirable, it is not necessarily the right answer for *every* church. The help of your experts is invaluable here, though the size of the chancel must be one of the determining factors.

6. There is, on the face of it, much to be said for a West end organ, provided the choir is there as well. The problems of a chancel choir and a West end organ keeping together are considerable, especially for the unfortunate congregation sitting plumb in the middle of both parties.

7. Over the years an organist may have become accustomed to the sound of a boxed-in chancel organ and the muffled effect which ensues when perhaps three sides of the instrument speak directly on to a wall. The same instrument is likely to produce entirely different sounds when placed in an open position in the body of the church. Frequently, under the new conditions, the organist does not realise that he must play much more softly than before if he is not literally to blast choir and congregation out of the building. He is usually far too obsessed with the big noise he can make on his new toy.

8. Organists are equally preoccupied with what they believe to be the status symbol of having a detached console. In most churches this is not necessary, though the organist may hoodwink the P.C.C. by convincing them of the need for this expensive luxury. It is surely more important to spend money on tonal improvements; the ultimate sounds which an organ will produce should always be the principal objective.

9. Organists will invariably go to the stake over electric action, another expensive proposition. They often forget (conveniently?) that modern tracker action, while being much lighter than the cumbersome mechanics to be found in most 19th century organs, is far less likely to go wrong. The element of key resistance which it provides also has the merit of a contact with the pipe which can never be realised to the same extent with electric action.

10. Many clergy and P.C.C.'s are at first understandably frightened off at the prospect of having to raise many hundreds of pounds for work on the organ. Experience repeatedly shows how quickly the money is likely to come in when a concerted effort by the parish, directed in many ways, produces amazing results.

11. To the man in the pew, a renovated organ often sounds little or no different from what it did before, though the organist will be aware of the improvement when playing it. As donors always like to see something for their money, remember the psychological effect of cleaning the organ case and regilding the pipes.

12. As mentioned earlier, resist what on the face of it might appear to be the temptation to have an electronic instrument. Only seriously consider this if your church is too small for even the smallest of pipe organs or if you are in the Tropics where the high rate of humidity, or insects, will ruin a pipe organ in no time.

13. A piano can sound very fine in a church. It has much to commend it and it will often be much easier to find a pianist than an organist. In churches overseas where a piano is used for accompanying the services, gramophone records of orchestral music are sometimes played as voluntaries.

THE RÔLE OF THE CONGREGATION

The conception of the congregation as a fully involved worshipping community is a legitimate one. This is now being accepted everywhere, even in cathedrals where the tradition—or myth—that the congregation remain dumb is often being forcibly exploded. How important then is the value of this in a parish church where a different set of conditions usually prevails.

One of the most striking aspects of the experimental Series Two Communion Service is its demand for involvement. In the "togetherness" which is at the root of the new liturgy there is an active role for *everyone,* be they clergy, servers, choir or congregation. The congregation must therefore fulfil their obligations and play their part to the best of their ability. As the choir, bell ringers and servers practise, so then must the congregation. If this seems a new departure, the wisdom of "doing all things well" is an admirable maxim which should always be uppermost in our minds. We are always being told, or tell others, that only the best will do in the service of God and although it may be querulous to define a uniform ideal as to what is best, the idea of doing all things well is something which can be readily understood by all.

If a congregation is to fulfill its role to the best of its ability—and this is often potentially much greater than is at first deemed to be possible—it must of necessity practise from time to time. Only by doing so can it improve its contribution to the services as well as being shown where it may be going wrong.

It will generally be best if the practices take the place of a sermon rather than be imposed on the congregation as an extra either before or after a service. Most parsons will anyhow be only too glad to be relieved of preparing a sermon once in a while.

Various factors will decide who is the person best suited to conduct a congregational choir practice. The organist of the church may not necessarily be the obvious choice as this is in the nature of specialist work. Helped and encouraged by the right person, a congregation can be made to enjoy themselves to such an extent that they will sing far better than ever before. Similarly, in the hands of the wrong person, the attempt can meet with such dire and unforgettable results that there will seldom, if ever, be an opportunity for a second attempt.

In the end, whoever conducts such a rehearsal must remember that most congregations are likely to view the project initially with some suspicion. The personality of whoever is in charge may not entirely allay their suspicions but may at least persuade them to want to come back for more. Once the congregation sees the reasons for rehearsing and then the progressive results of its labours, the chances are that they will become keen to improve more and more.

On these occasions it is important that the congregation sit together rather than scattered in ones and twos all over the church. People who are loth to vacate the isolated seat they have occupied for the past forty years are not going to be of much practical help when it comes to this particular aspect of corporate worship. As, for reasons best known to themselves, there is often staunch opposition to sitting in the front rows of the pews, it is wisest to suggest that the people sit together, as a group, in the middle of the church. It is doubtful whether they will ever be persuaded of the wisdom of permanently sitting together.

In addition to being the ideal occasions for introducing and learning new hymns—and that means new words as well as new tunes—these rehearsals can be useful for getting a number of points across to the congregation. If possible, there ought also to be an opportunity for questions; this helps the congregation to feel that they have had their money's worth.

Time ought also to be allowed for rehearsing the said parts of the services in which everyone is meant to join. As most congregations and many choirs mumble their way through these parts, there is every reason to try to improve this aspect of worship.

There seems to be an unwritten tradition, as mentioned in Chapter Nine, that when in church one adopts, for some unknown reason, an unnatural voice; this means that we speak in a style which is parsonical, affected or plain dreary. A bishop, in speaking of one of his clergy, was once heard to remark "He makes the Gospel sound the dullest news on earth". Corporate worship, especially when it happens to be the good news of the Gospel, ought always to sound interesting. There is no excuse for being dull. Congregations need to be periodically reminded not only of this but of such essential niceties as commas and general phrasing; this applies especially in the all-too-familiar Creed, Lesser Litany and Lord's Prayer. Observance of punctuation helps to produce an intelligent result which is far removed from the gabbled free-for-all which is too frequently part and parcel of our services.

In this respect it is so seldom remembered that speaking in any large building, either individually or in groups, demands a more deliberate enunciation than when speaking informally in a small room. There must never be any undue sense of hurry, for this only serves to destroy much of the spacious beauty of the prose of the liturgy (see page 95).

In the end it is the necessarily repetitive nature of the content of much of our services which demands an effort of concentration and thought. Each member of the congregation ought to try to discover a new meaning in familiar words each time they are spoken aloud or sung. This will demand much from those involved but it helps to avoid parrot-fashion recitation and it encourages vitality. Surely this is not too much to demand of our worship?

IMPROVISATION

Most organists attempt to improvise or "to make up the music as they go along" for two reasons:

1. Because it is the lazy man's way out from the labour of preparing set voluntaries, and

2. As some organists have the gift for doing it easily (and making it sound so effortless), others who are less gifted think they can do the same and follow suit.

Improvising is in fact one of the most highly specialised branches of practical music.

On the continent it is generally viewed with such importance as to become one of the priorities in the training of organists. Here in England we merely dabble in it and seldom take it seriously. As we do so little about teaching it, we can have little cause to complain about what we so frequently have to put up with. The wise organist who knows he cannot improvise does not attempt it in anything but the smallest doses. Others, who do not realise their inability, inflict on their congregations the most diabolical sounds.

With so much organ music of every possible type available today, with or without pedals, easy or difficult, there is little need for an organist to improvise unless he can do it really well; not, one hastens to add, because he thinks he does it well but because he has been told so by people who know.

The desirability of the organ being used to cover up every moment of what otherwise would be silence is questionable. There are, however, places in most services where a few well chosen bars of music add something in atmosphere. These are the places when improvising is generally best suited to the occasion as even the shortest of pieces is likely to be too long. The most obvious places for this are

1. In those churches where, at the Eucharist, there is a Gospel procession. Quiet music is needed to cover the move back to the Altar in preparation for the Creed.

2. At the end of the Offertory Hymn, if this is not long enough for the collection to have been brought up. (The need for music here would seldom be necessary if the hymn chosen was of the right length.

3. At the conclusion of a service, a few bars of quiet music as the choir and clergy leave the stalls. This is usually more tasteful than launching into a loud voluntary immediately after the Blessing when the congregation may be saying their private devotions.

These then are legitimate places for improvising. How should one go about it? The need for simplicity and a sense of shape ought fundamentally to be at the root of any improvising. The almost exclusive use of quasi hymn tune four part harmony is too derivative and difficult to sustain convincingly for any length of time. It is made the more so when the pedals are used unceasingly and usually in the lower octave of the pedal board. This sort of thing is unimaginative and soon palls on the ear, especially when the player meanders on in an all too familiar pattern which gives little thought to key, time or melodic outline.

The keyboard needs to be exploited; two part harmony, one hand on each manual, can with a little thought weave some delicate tracery. Many efforts at improvising never seem to get away from the middle of the keyboard while the choice of stops could seldom be termed adventurous. The use of a distinctive rhythm as the basis of an improvisation ought also to be considered. There are many permutations of rhythm, key and time which organists seldom if ever explore, merely because they do not take the trouble of working something out in their minds before they begin.

Improvising is not meandering

Some of the best examples can be heard in cathedrals where the organists, often through years of experience and self-criticism may well produce very worthwhile miniatures based on a phrase from a chant or anthem being sung during the service. Those who heard Sir Edward Bairstow at York Minster will remember how artistically he did this sort of thing. His sense of originality, plus more than a smattering of genius, was at the root not only of his improvising but of almost everything he did.

Unless you are a born genius at this sort of thing, practise your improvising for a long time in private before you come out with it in public. Even then, you will have off days—who doesn't? The end product can only be judged on whether it is musical or not. Do bear in mind that an inability to improvise well is not necessarily a reflection on your musicianship. It is far too often taken for granted that organists must of necessity be improvisers. Only a relatively few musicians are natural improvisers; of the rest only a handful can do it with any degree of skill—so take heart!

CONDUCTING

From time to time most organists have to conduct. Whether it be the directing of the simplest of unaccompanied anthems or the most complicated of modern scores, certain basic principles, as in improvising, are called for. These are to be found in any handbook on the subject, many of which have useful explanatory diagrams. (See Appendix 16).

A few points require emphasising. The first need is for a clear beat which can be understood by all. A series of hand flappings in which each successive beat is identical in looks—and has no beginning or end—is nothing but a hindrance to all concerned with trying to follow it. The preparation, giving the singers time to take breath, is necessary. Similarly, the "cut off" at the end must be preceded by a preparatory warning movement if everyone is to stop singing unanimously. If, when conducting, you find the choir's attack is untidy and the final consonants ragged, this may be because your beat is not as clear an indication as it should be. Conductors who are quick to call their choirs to account over untidy singing, often have only themselves to blame for giving such unrhythmic and flabby indications.

The excesses of gesticulation and arm-waving, often accompanied by hideous grimaces, which constitute some people's efforts at conducting, are of no avail and seldom help in achieving musical results, even though they may gratify the person responsible. In church a simple, but rhythmic, movement of the hand, or even the finger, is much more to the point. It is also less obtrusive to the congregation. The more fussy the hand movement, the less likelihood will there be of the singers watching it—or understanding it. Amateur conductors are seldom aware how distracting their antics can be to the onlooker.

Decide the *tempo* before you start. Many are the conductors who, having begun at a speed which they realise to be wrong, attempt to right it by altering the pace—and then cursing the choir for raggedness. If you hit on a wrong speed you must either cut your losses and keep to it or *very* gradually ease the pulse into the correct tempo.

The old idea of learning how to beat time by looking at your efforts in a mirror has much to commend it, if you agree to be self-critical and not automatically to imagine yourself as a second Barbirolli.

The use of the right hand is ideally sufficient in itself. The left hand fulfils no useful purpose if it merely mirrors what the right hand is doing. If you use the left hand, do so to indicate specific points, such as crescendos and diminuendos, or to give a lead in to one of the parts. It must be stressed that unnecessary movement, especially if you are in a chancel and visible to all, distracts the listener's attention away from the music and from the business of worship.

RECITALS AND SPECIAL SERVICES

These are admirable "extras" provided the preparation for them is also undertaken as an extra commitment. The routine rehearsing of the Sunday music must never be allowed to suffer, no matter how tempting may be the prospect of devoting much of the normal rehearsal time to new and perhaps exciting music.

Christmas and Easter are obvious occasions for such ventures, with a galaxy of appropriate music to choose from. Non-liturgical services, based on the King's College, Cambridge pattern of lessons and carols continue to hold a fatal fascination for choirs and congregations alike. The R.S.C.M.'s collection of Easter music, *Risen with Christ,* contains nineteen carefully contrasted anthems and hymns. Passiontide is also an obvious time for performing works such as Charles Wood's *Passion according to St. Mark* and Somervell's *Passion of Christ.*

If, for one reason or another, a choir cannot put on an entire programme, there is much to commend, on certain occasions, a twenty minute programme of music in place of the sermon at Evensong. Nor should the linking up of neighbouring choirs be overlooked; a couple of choirs who thus join forces can do much to stimulate interest and promote relationships. The conducting and playing can be shared between the respective organists. If the congregations of both churches are encouraged to support such a venture, so much the better.

Occasions of this nature can often be treated as a useful preliminary to a Deanery Choral Festival. In the Exeter Diocese a number of such events are held each year in various parishes; these in their turn lead up to the Diocesan Choral Festival in the cathedral. Other dioceses no doubt have similar arrangements.

Secular concerts can provide a pleasant distraction from the continuous round of music performed in church. As such they can help to broaden the musical outlook of the choir and often reveal unsuspected and otherwise hidden talents in many individuals. Whatever form a recital may take, the chances are that it will help to further good relationships between the choir and the congregation. It will be the more acceptable if the standard of performance is so high as to make the audience really proud of their choir's efforts.

The planning of any programme needs to be carefully thought out. Points to bear in mind are:

1. *Length.* Hard pews make anything lasting more than an hour into an endurance test in which attention becomes diverted towards bodily comforts. A hymn, strategically placed in the middle of the programme, gives members of the congregation a chance to stretch their legs and air their lungs. It is far better for listeners to go away wanting more rather than relieved at having endured—bravely or otherwise—a much longer spell while vowing, into the bargain, never to come again.
2. Never be encouraged, for any reason, to choose music which proves to be beyond the capabilities of the choir. Simple music well sung is a joy to the listener while difficult music inadequately performed is, or should be, an embarrassment to all concerned.
3. The programme content should be varied. The interest for the listener is the greater when choral music is followed by some organ music, and *vice versa.*

GETTING ON WITH EVERYONE AND ENTERING INTO THE LIFE OF THE PARISH

Civilisation is, and always has been, cluttered with the debris both of relationships which have gone wrong and with unresolved personal quarrels. Although the Church's business is that of worshipping God and saving souls—two admirable occupations—those who comprise the Church are nevertheless human. As such, they are no less susceptible to human virtues or prone to human failings than anyone else.

It must be allowed that working for the Church can do something to a person; his manner and his dealings with other people can, as a result, prove unrealistic and unbusinesslike. This, in some measure, may be a cultivated pose but more likely to reflect an aspect of the 19th century Barchester-like façade which still patchily exists.

As a race, the organists of today are generally more sociable than they were at one time. Even so, much of this only comes to the fore in restricted ways such as when two or more get together to discuss wind pressures and leathered diapasons. On these occasions eyes light up and an instant means of brotherly communication is established.

Matters are not helped when organists and choirs take little or no part in the life of the parish apart from what they contribute musically. There still exists a school of thought which proudly asserts that the music is the only thing of any concern in worship. The attitude of the organist interested solely in music and who by-passes being either a practising or communicating Christian, is likely to be quickly reflected in his playing and probably even more so in the work of his choir.

Many organists spend most of their church life at the console, purposely choosing to be isolated from contact with the life of the parish whereas, because of his position and the nature of his work, he ought if anything to be more deeply committed to the full Christian life than the man in the pew.

The organist who takes the trouble to know his congregation—and that will include most of the members of the P.C.C.—will find that it can pay handsome dividends, for it will give him the opportunity of discussing his problems and, if he so wishes, of doing some surruptitious lobbying. When the time comes for a decision on rebuilding the organ or increasing the organist's salary, the P.C.C. are the more likely to be forthcoming if they really know their organist instead of distantly viewing him from the body of the church as a slightly unknown quantity.

If you have a row with your Vicar, your choir or your P.C.C. (even the most placid of people find themselves sometimes drawn into quarrels), don't sulk. Having had your quarrel, whether you were in the right or the wrong, whether you won it or lost it—forget it. Always remember that in any community, even that of the Church, we all have to learn to live with one another, so we must endeavour to make the best of it.

WIDENING YOUR VISION

Listen to all the music you possibly can, be it live, on the radio or on records. Never, in the entire history of musical endeavour have there been such opportunities for hearing music as there are today.

While it is highly desirable that organists learn much from listening to organ music through any of these mediums, it is through the more diverse fields of music that knowledge, perception and critical values can be best widened. These faculties, having once been acquired, benefit the work of a church musician. Listening to chamber music can be a great help towards the playing of Bach's organ music. The four-fold partnership of a string quartet can suggest much that is helpful in articulating Bach's contrapuntal texture. Orchestral music can teach us much in relation to the mixing of instrumental colour; this in its turn can be applied to organ registration and helps us to make the best use of the available stops.

Hearing and observing first-rate singers, either individually or in choral groups, can provide material help on points concerning vocal technique, style and interpretation. Listening to performances by good choral societies or, better still, attending their rehearsals, are other ways of acquiring help to widen one's outlook and vision. As an organist never knows when he may be asked to conduct a choral society, a prior knowledge of the know-how is invaluable.

The work of the R.S.C.M. has been dealt with in Chapter 8. Making the best use of the courses they arrange for organists and choirmasters is yet another way of increasing practical knowledge. This knowledge helps to increase the skill of the individual. Using to the full every opportunity of hearing performances of church music by first rate choirs is an experience not to be missed. The wide range of recorded music now available will meet most needs in this direction.

Finally, reading everything possible concerning musical matters can be both a stimulus and an inspiration. Musical periodicals provide a wealth of information contained in special articles, reviews and concert notices, all of which help to keep one up to date with current trends and in touch with what is generally taking place. This widening of vision should be one of the main objectives for the church musician. Too often the narrow and often inhibited field of organs and church music contrive to claim our attention to the virtual exclusion of the wider and all-embracing aspect. The church musician who is well versed on every possible angle of music will be the richer musician. This is what ultimately matters.

SOME OBSERVATIONS ON THE CHURCH AND ITS MUSIC OVERSEAS

In my travels overseas I have seen many parallels with the problems we are experiencing in this country. Because of the prevailing local conditions in most of these distant lands, the Church has to contend with a formidable shortage of personnel. The potential from which to recruit will continue to diminish as our presence in what was once the British Empire continues to be less and less.

The church overseas has to make do, often as best it can, to a much greater extent than in this country. Perhaps, because of this, its enforced reliability on itself produces hidden reserves of strength; what I saw of the Anglican church in the Far East and India, and to a certain extent in Africa, left me in little doubt as to its vitality and highly charged witness. Why is this so? It is first and foremost a minority church functioning in basically non-Christian, though far from non-religious, countries. It is essentially a missionary church often having to fight for its means of existence, or even for its survival. From this it derives much of its strength and impact.

In its history the Church overseas is, by comparison with England, so young. Perhaps it is because of this that it is much more geared to thinking in terms of the future than we generally are. It is certainly more concerned with pastoral care than with maintaining tradition for its own sake. One of our paradoxical traditions in England is the superabundance of Sunday services with our congregations spread out in relatively small numbers, the members of each persuasion clinging, often with persistence, to what they were brought up to and only very reluctantly changing ships in mid-stream. So much for our inherent conservatism! In the East, especially in India, I found that the eggs are nearly always put into one basket—the Parish Communion—often followed by a communal breakfast. This is invariably the only morning service and, as such, has rapidly assumed the importance which rightly attaches to it. Add to this the fact that there are far fewer churches and you have, time and again, services packed to capacity.

All these factors, because they are challenging, produce vigour and are reflected in the music which I repeatedly found to be very sincere although it was often lacking in polish. The standard of achievement was the more remarkable when one considers the extent to which they are denied opportunities for hearing live music as a model, something we at home tend to take for granted, possibly because it is so readily accessible to us.

It is difficult to define in so many words the ingredients which so often constitute the Anglican Church in distant lands. Certain factors, some of them local, helped to point the way, not the least the generally forward looking spirit of adventure and experiment though there were pockets of innate conservatism, much the same as there are here in this country. Even so, I found the Church generally much less suspicious of change than we are and I soon became forcibly aware of the identification of the Church with the people to a far greater extent than is so often the case here.

On the practical side, bearing in mind distance and inaccessibility, what was said earlier (Chapter 8) on ways and means of acquiring help apply in even greater measure to the Church overseas. The value there of R.S.C.M. affiliation, if only for the purposes of keeping in touch with what is going on, cannot be overstressed.

12 The future?

> If we want things to stay as they are, things will have to change.
>
> *Tancredi:* THE LEOPARD

> It is unwillingness to accept change, and the feeling of insecurity which this unwillingness reflects....
>
> *Tibor Barna:* INVESTMENT AND GROWTH POLICIES IN BRITISH INDUSTRIAL FIRMS

> Churches become attached to trivial things, and do not like to have them altered.
>
> *Stephen Neill:* ANGLICANISM

We are living in an age of tremendous and far-reaching change which, in the Church, is altering the structure of worship. The very nature of the establishment is even in question.

These changes, whether we like them or not, are inevitable; they are very necessary to the witness and vigour of the Church, possibly even for its very survival. For many of us there is an instinctive fear of exchanging what we know for the unknown. This does not apply solely to matters concerning the Church but is part of the inherent conservatism which has become built-in to the British way of life. As such, it is both a blessing and a bane.

For most of us, church-going is a very comfortable process which acts as a sort of minor narcotic, for it leaves us with a feeling of well-being plus some degree of self-satisfaction. Many of us allow our religion to demand little more of us than is absolutely necessary. In a nutshell, most of us if we are honest must admit to living in a complacent ecclesiastical museum. From time to time we need substantial jolts, a major example of which is taking place within the Church today. What is happening will—and must—alter our attitude to much of the historical background to worship which has been taken for granted for so long. In the process of the contemporary upheaval, could it be that the Church is running down so that it can be built up again with renewed zest, relevant to the day and age in which we live? This sequence of events is not without its parallel in the past and may well be a manifestation of the Holy Spirit working within us.

THE NEW LOOK

One of the dangers of the revolution—or reformation—of liturgical processes now taking place is that once started it could conceivably become difficult to control. As with any revolution or major upheaval the zeal of the reformers can easily get out of hand. There is a very real danger that in our commendable enthusiasm to get rid of archaic language (together with its attendant problems) and redundant traditions, we shall be "doing a Beeching" by throwing out too much so that the baby will disappear with the bath water.

Allan Wicks, organist of Canterbury Cathedral, has spoken of the dangers of what he terms "instant communication"—the contemporary trend, both within the Church and in the world at large, which seeks to present everything as too easily and too readily ours without any real effort being necessary on our part. An Exeter priest, in speaking of people making their communion, recently wrote in his parish magazine "There are too many people today who wish to stride up to their Maker and shake hands as with an equal". In other words, the "ideal" (?) permeating many walks of life that we have the *right* to expect that everything should be handed to us "on a plate". Is there a subtle reflection here, subconsciously or otherwise, of the welfare state?

In the process, the distinctions between sacred and secular are being ironed out to such an extent that we are in very real danger of losing two necessary ingredients to our worship—awe and mystery. Writing of the former in *Unread Best-seller—reflections on the Old Testament,* Dr. Mary Stocks says "He (Esdras II) knew the meaning of the word awe. He knew that it was the first condition of worship". By no means any less important is the need for a sense of reverence. It may be that we are witnessing a wholesale reaction to the sentiment which excessively charged much of the 19th century conception of sacredness, but we are nevertheless rapidly approaching the stage where little or nothing is left to the imagination of the worshipper, so obsessed are we with the belief that by bringing everything down to the lowest common denominator we shall draw more people into the Church. Artificial mateyness, together with the many stunts which form a prominent feature of certain sections of the Church today, merely serve to get people to church under false pretences. It is hard to believe that any degree of permanence is ever achieved through gimmicks—musical or otherwise—when they are presented as substitutes for spiritual values.

It is also abundantly clear that through a frightening lack of vision and personal conscience, we are very rapidly tending to lose sight of the fact that to do something well, be it praying, singing or, for that matter, anything to do with religion or with life in general, demands effort and discipline. If we by-pass these things we do so to our peril for they must in the end remain as essential components of worship. Perhaps Dr. Routley to some extent clinches the matter when he writes "The truth which needs to be emphasised in Protestant circles above all others, when Christian worship is under discussion, is that worship is essentially drama. Catholics have never really forgotten this, and there are vestiges of its recall in the worship of Anglicans."

Another aspect of the new look is seen in contemporary church architecture. While much of this may be admirable in relation to the functional demands of corporate worship and of "togetherness", the fact remains that little or nothing is left to the visual imagination. In this context the *raison d'etre* of the congregation gathered round a central altar in a round church is as obvious as the parallel with the "theatre in the round". In either case we absorb the whole at one glance and we feel (maybe) that "we belong". Such thinking has its virtues but also its drawbacks.

The symbolic design of a traditional cruciform church leads the eye onwards—often unexpectedly—from one vista to another and from one level to another, culminating in the high altar which is in every respect the centre piece. Here then are two opposing views of visual aids to worship; neither is necessarily completely right or wrong.

Out of this welter of re-thinking emerges the question of the place which music should occupy both in its own right and contributory to the scheme of things.

THE NEW TYPES OF MUSIC EMERGING FROM THE CHANGE IN THOUGHT TODAY

With so much concentration of energies on congregational participation, it is hardly surprising that there is much discussion concerning hymns. It may be that our musical perception is at the present time more critical and searching than ever before but we have suddenly woken up to the fact that many of our favourite and time-honoured hymns contain poor music while the words demand even closer scrutiny. Much of what we sing about, which we now realise to be theologically shaky or even doubtful, is more often than not stated clumsily and re-echoes sentiments which present little valid prospect of what the Christian faith is concerned with.

The new thought in hymn writing can be best summed up in two distinct phases:

1. Words and music in a "traditional" (for want of a better word) style, though reflecting in no small measure a strength and sincerity of purpose which is far removed from most of our Victorian favourites. The choice is quite considerable and certain examples are given in Appendix 17.

2. The exciting "new look" as seen, for example, in the works of Sydney Carter, the finest and certainly the most popular of which is probably *The Lord of the Dance*. Galliard Ltd., Queen

Anne's Road, Southtown, Great Yarmouth, Norfolk. Here are words of tremendously gripping intensity which speak in a language readily understood by all; the immediate impact of the verse about Good Friday is forceful and straight to the point:

I danced on a Friday
When the sky turned black—
It's hard to dance
With the devil on your back.
They buried my body
And they thought I'd gone—
But I am the dance
And I still go on.

Dance then wherever you may be,
I am the Lord of the Dance, said he,
And I'll lead you all, wherever you may be,
And I'll lead you all in the dance, said he.

The folk song to which these words are set is no less attractive and the resultant marrying of words and music is complete, with the one complementing the other. One would presume to forecast that the introduction of more hymns of this nature would do much in helping to assure a healthy outlook for the future of our hymnody.

The music of Malcolm Williamson is in some respects a runner up, though the quality of his collection *12 New Hymn Tunes,* (published by Josef Weinberger Ltd., 33 Crawford Street, London. W.1.). is unequal. *Hail to the Lord who comes* is the best; it has a sense of purpose which adds to the stamina of the words but is spoilt by the harmonies of the final bars. Williamson's *Procession of Palms,* although a much more extended work, speaks in a forceful and direct language.

The psalmody of Joseph Gélineau (see Chapter 3) is in many respects a break through in the attempt to overcome some of the many difficulties which beset the traditional Anglican method of psalm singing. One of the chief virtues of Gélineau's approach is the variety of ways in which each psalm can be sung. The folk music style employed for the chants is highly attractive and has helped towards ensuring the popularity in many quarters of this novel and worthwhile scheme.

THE "POP" ELEMENT

While folk music has its roots in the same sort of historical background as that from which our liturgy grew, "pop" is a thoroughly alien importation and a self-conscious parasite. "Pop", together with the incidental noise and ironmongery which seems to be a necessary part of its presentation, can be quickly dismissed as an irrelevant and mercifully transient stunt. Dr. Routley's pointed comments on the subject were quoted in Chapter 4.

Though the intentions of the 20th Century Church Light Music Group are in no way suspect, what has materialised is, for the most part, shallow, sugary and full of type-cast endings and clichés. While the rhythmic content is often more easily acceptable than the consistent harmonic weakness, most of the compositions coming from this group savour, at their worst, of music hall style while at their best they might be described as the Sankey and Moody of today.

In referring to the Group, David Holbrook writing in *The Musical Times* of April 1964, says "In every other characteristic these devotional songs date back to the cruder manifestations of music and poetry of about seventy years ago, when people first seemed to become aware of the possibilities of deliberately exploiting bad taste".

Whatever changes come our way, or are forced on us, there is a pressing need for music to be written for country choirs and organists with limited resources and techniques. Up to now the more fortunately placed cathedral and collegiate choirs have had most of the icing on the cake. The best composers of church music could now perform a valuable service to country churches by writing music tailored to the resources available in the smaller parishes. Composers such as Britten, Ridout and Alan Gibbs are writing music for children's choirs; the simple and for the most part diatonic style they employ, together with reasonably straightforward organ accompaniments, is a move in the right direction. One of the hopes for the future is that more and more secular composers should write for the church; brought up in an environment essentially other than church music, they are bringing a fresh outlook to what can so easily be a restricted field of composition. At the present time we generally have either so much contemporary music which, secular and religious alike, is difficult to sing and play, or else a conglomeration of utilitarian music, much of it unbelievably shoddy, lacking in musicianship or plain dull. In between these extremes there is far too little to choose from.

Composers might also bear in mind the problems created through the present scarcity of organists, a situation which is not likely to improve very much in the foreseeable future. Accompaniments for instruments other than the organ, even to the extent of using on occasion school orchestras, might well be considered by composers as a feasible proposition. The organ is not the *only* instrument for church use.

THE MUSIC AND MUSICIANS MUST BE READILY ADAPTABLE TO THE NEEDS OF THE FUTURE

Much heart searching is needed. We must look realistically to the future while taking along with us the best, and only the best, of both the past and the present. There is sometimes too much wanting to put the clock back, to live nostalgically and sentimentally in the past—"the old tunes are good enough for me" attitude.

To some of us, much of the music of our time is often strange and even incomprehensible, yet there must always be new thought and experiment, both within and without the Church. It must also be remembered that modern words in a 20th century context generally have a more ready appeal to modern man than to the older generation weaned on a more archaic type of ecclesiastical language. Whether or not the latter is understood is apparently immaterial to some people.

In looking to the future we organists might take more advantage of the practical aids now so readily available. The ever-increasing issue of long playing records of church and organ music is a teaching aid such as our forebears never knew and is something we cannot afford to ignore. We must also be very aware of the pastoral implications of all that we do and of the responsibility which thus devolves upon us. We must see to it that our music will lift us up. It must compel men to *want* to worship and in doing so to make worship the more real and meaningful.

THE INCREASING RÔLE OF THE CONGREGATION

This has been frequently mentioned elsewhere in this book for it is a potent sign of the times. The reasons why congregational singing is likely to assume a major rôle in corporate worship have all been discussed at some length. A tradition—and a healthy one at that—has yet to be firmly established for it must be remembered that congregational participation, in terms of the Communion Service and contemporary hymnody, is a comparatively recent innovation.

Looking then to the future, the rôle of the congregation, if it is to be effective, must not be the half-hearted affair which is all that it is in some churches, nor must it assume a noisome proportion of parrot-fashion bawling, helped on its way by an excess of heartiness. All this applies equally to what is said as well as to what is sung. In this direction there is much yet to be learnt and we must always be aware of the rightful application of the congregation's part in our services. Participation is a measure of the "togetherness" which is the watchword of the Church today.

THE NEED FOR OUR WILLINGNESS TO GO ALONG WITH ALL THIS

Much will depend on our personal attitude. How many of us really want to see a new dimension to the witness and worship of the Church? How many of us are afraid of facing the future, afraid because what we know is personally more secure than the uncertainty of the unknown, exciting though that could well be.

In the fullness of time the emerging pattern of events will

determine the future of the Church. The faint-hearted will either be swept along by the force generated by the tide of events, musical or otherwise, or be left stranded high and dry. Ideally, we ought to approach the future with confidence, each of us playing his or her full part. The challenge of the future could well prove to be the strength of the Church provided we do not allow our present preoccupation with liturgical reform to become such an obsession that it overshadows spiritual processes. There is already a danger of this which could result so easily with the cart being put before the horse.

Our sense of vision then must be wide but it must also be all-embracing; it must be forward looking but taking in, *en route,* the best of the past (and it must be reiterated again that there is much of this).

Above all, we must have faith in an age where God still moves in a mysterious way, surprising though this may seem. The final word on the future seems to lie with the writer of the book of Proverbs when he tells us that "Where there is no vision the people perish". This is our challenge and it is not only the people but the Church which today stands in danger of perishing.

13 Conclusions

> How far is church music necessary to the well-being of the contemporary church? It has to be answered in full recognition of the secularisation of society which is one of the great new facts of our time.
>
> Churchmen . . . are shy of attaching any importance to the notion that in worship "we" are doing anything at all. . . . What matters is to persuade the Protestant worshipper that he is doing something.
>
> *Erik Routley:* WORDS, MUSIC AND THE CHURCH

WHAT IS DEMANDED OF US AS CHURCH ORGANISTS?

1. We are *all* capable of much better results than most of us in fact ever achieve, therefore much is rightly demanded of us and we need to be much more self-critical of the results of our labours. We are too ready to make excuses for our sins of omission and in doing so we become party to the slipshod attitudes which all too often prevail in the conduct of the services. Much of our church music tradition is bedevilled by apathy, complacency and smugness. One of the major failings of the Church is this inability—in certain quarters—to perceive the importance of doing all things well and of getting the priorities sorted out. The so called "state" appearance at church of royalty, judges and mayors is more likely than not to draw forth a greater degree of fuss and reverence than is sometimes meted out to the Almighty!

2. The British tradition of amateur music-making, of which church choirs are an important part, is something unique and of which we are rightly proud; but, being amateur is no excuse

for permitting low, or even downright bad, standards. The comparison with the high standards achieved in many other fields of musical activity can be embarrassing and at times even odious. Playing off professional and amateur elements against each other matters not one scrap. Each must be judged in its own right. What matters is sincerity of purpose and "cutting one's cloth" etc. rather than attempting to compete.

3. The need for simple but attractive music has been mentioned in the previous chapter. There is also the need for choirmasters to be forward looking and to make some attempt at coming to terms with contemporary thought instead of contemptuously dismissing out of hand anything in a modern idiom. Victoriana, good or bad, holds an almost exclusively magnetic lure for so many.

4. To those really conscientious choirmasters and organists who do all in their power to strive for first rate results one would say, do not despair. The fact that all of us do despair from time to time may be some comfort! It does point at some effort being made towards an awareness of standards. What ultimately matters is integrity of purpose; it will demand much in time and effort and will produce much in the way of disappointments, for we are human beings dealing with human beings.

5. There is a constant need for our reassessment of the psychological approach necessary to our relationships with each other within the Church.

6. We must always be on the look-out for ways and means of obtaining help which will increase efficiency and contribute towards a businesslike approach to all musical matters. At all costs, we must avoid the dangers of parochialism and isolation.

7. We must always grasp the opportunity to help in training someone else to take our place. In this, we shall be doing the Church a great service; never before in the history of church music has the succession been more questionable or problematic than it is today.

8. We should always seek to instil in our choir members the

implication of being part of a voluntary organisation. The only part which is voluntary is the individual decision to join; thereafter it should be a matter of complete commitment through loyal and unswerving support.

The popular image of the Church more often than not appears to the man in the street as something archaic and out of touch with reality. The fortunes—or perhaps the misfortunes—of the Church's inheritance have done much to foster this conception of a quasi-monastic institution generally unidentified with, and even on occasion seen to be unconcerned with, or for, people. The fact that the Church seems to attract its share of oddities and cranks, though possibly no more or less than in other walks of life today, is in part responsible for whatever image the Church projects. It is, in fact, often unfairly taken for granted that clergy and organists will be slightly "off beam" and because of this they are easy prey for caricature—and sometimes not without justification.

Just how far the Church should readjust itself to the day and age in which we live, without losing essential principles, is one of the great problems confronting it at the present time. Arising out of this is a sense of general restlessness while much is in a state of flux. Spasmodic outbursts come from the most unexpected quarters; a dean's descent by parachute, wine and cheese parties in the nave and a fashion show in the crypt bring us back with a bump to square one. Such frivolities mystify those on the touch line while, for the paid-up members, they provide light relief not to be taken seriously.

While the best of the Church's traditions are invaluable and will outlive any form of gimmickry, the worst of its traditions are trivial, irrelevant and best discarded. When all is said and done we cannot live on a diet made up almost exclusively either of traditions or stunts, in either instance at the expense of reality. The well-intentioned clamour for reform within the Church so often finds itself linked with the line of thought which sees ceremonial, in any shape or guise, as an unnecessary encumbrance. This reflects but one of the dangers which the wholesale abandonment of personal discipline today brings in its wake. This is true not only of the Church but of all walks of life.

The work of the Liturgical Commission is most widely known for the experimental Series Two Liturgy in which a very real attempt has been made to maintain the best of the old side by side with new material. It is only to be expected that not everyone would agree with the relevance of this new look for it is in its infant days and we are anyhow rooted in centuries of ecclesiastical conservatism, much of it turgid and heavily biased towards any form of innovation.

If we do not experiment, we and the Church run the very real risk of becoming moribund and even more apathetic than we are today. Beautiful in its own right though much of the 17th century language of the Book of Common Prayer may be, it is as we become more and more accustomed to the wording of Series Two that many of us are made forcibly aware, in retrospect, of Cranmer's "wordy" phraseology. As an example of this, Cranmer's Confession in the Communion Service and that used in Series Two make for interesting comparison. It is not merely a question of relative length, or of whether we use, or do not use, "thou" and "thee". More to the point is the basic means of communication which must be uppermost in our minds, whether or not it is relevant to 1662 or, much more important, to the age in which we live. People come to church to hear the word of God and not to listen to the reading of Elizabethan English.

Our vision is the challenge of the future. In this future, church music and church musicians have a vital role to play, hand in hand with, yet complementary to, the evangelistic work of the Church. Each one of us must search his or her conscience and all of us must renew our effort so that we contribute something of worth to the kingdom of God. In doing so we shall be helping to re-vitalize the witness of the Church. We must believe utterly and completely the relevance of what we sing, even perhaps bearing in mind Shakespeare's injunction that "words without thoughts never to heaven go". We must also accept the diversities of gifts of which St. Paul reminds us. Each of us has something to give, no matter how humble this may be, but each according to the gifts which the good God in his wisdom has bestowed on us.

"See what thou singest with thy mouth, thou believest in thy heart, and what thou believest in thy heart thou dost confirm by thy deeds."

Because of his immense scholarship and vision, I have frequently quoted Dr. Routley. The last word must also lie with him:

> 'We know a great deal, we feel a great deal, and we are passionately concerned for the future—concerned the more because it has never been so doubtful whether we have a future. . . . The church's concern for beauty will never prosper unless the concerns for truth and beauty are kept running. . . . These are the greatest days for church music since the 16th century, and for exactly the same historical reason; the wheel of history has come round again. The danger is part of the adventure."

Appendices

APPENDIX 1. *Hymn books for parish churches*

Hymns A & M Revised 1950 (Clowes). A "middle-of-the-road" collection which cut out the disused material of Hymns A & M Standard and substituted newer material which had become popular between 1900 and 1950. Additional is *100 Hymns for To-day* (Clowes, 1969).

Anglican Hymn Book (Church Book Room Press). A generous collection with music from a wide range, still retaining something of the evangelical character of the book (*Church Hymnal for the Christian Year*) it replaced. See also *Hymns and Songs* (Epworth).

The English Hymnal (OUP). Appeals particularly to a musically-cultured and liturgically-conscious congregation.

English Hymnal Service Book (OUP). A collection of quite a different character from that of *English Hymnal,* having a limited number of carefully-selected hymns and carols, together with music for Morning and Evening Prayer, Holy Communion (Merbecke), and a simply pointed psalter (without chants), all under one cover.

Two recent books of special musical interest are the *BBC Hymn Book* (SPCK) and *Hymns for Church and School* (Novello). *The Cambridge Hymnal* (CUP) provides many interesting settings with a modern flavour, many of which could be used as simple anthems. The pop-style tunes of the 20th Century Church Light Music Group are published in collections and many of them are available on separate sheets (Weinberger). Good collections of modern religious songs, primarily intended for use with guitar accompaniment, are *Faith, Folk and Clarity* (for general use) and *Faith, Folk and Nativity* (for Christmas), also a collection of the carols of Sydney Carter and Donald Swann, all published by Galliard. *Sing Round the Year* (The Bodley Head), is another attractive collection of contemporary carols compiled by Donald Swann.

Appendix 2. *Psalters*

The Psalter Newly-Pointed (SPCK, 1925). A book that ensures good chanting by means of exacting rules and the use of a variety of symbols to show the pointing.

The Parish Psalter (Faith Press, 1928). A much simpler book than the above, widely used in parish churches. Its editor Sir Sydney Nicholson had congregations very much in mind.

The Worcester Psalter (A. & C. Black, 1950). Another simple psalter which can be recommended for parish church use.

The Revised Psalter (SPCK, 1966). The newly-worded authorised text is pointed in a simple manner resembling that of the *Parish Psalter.*

The Revised Parish Psalter (Faith Press, 1967). *The Revised Psalter* text and pointing together with chants.

Alternative Services Second Series, Morning & Evening Prayer (SPCK, ref: AS.210). Includes the Canticles as finally authorised for "Series II", pointed for singing.

For churches, chapels or schools where plainsong is used *A Manual of Plainsong* (Novello) or *The Plainchant Evening Psalter* (Plainchant Publications) is recommended. The latter includes the Evening Canticles and the Psalms appointed for Evening use.

Appendix 3. *Chant books*

The Anglican Chant Book (Novello). A good collection based on the chants most popularly used in cathedrals, large parish churches and schools.

St Nicolas Chant Book (Faith Press). Duplicates the chants which appear in the *Parish Psalter,* which were specially chosen for their low reciting-notes and general simplicity.

New Cathedral Psalter Chants (Novello). In three editions—No. 81 (one-star; also called *The St Paul's Cathedral Chant Book*) was designated "for cathedral use"; No. 82 (two-star) "for parish church use", and No. 83 (three-star) "for village church use". Lower reciting-notes and progressively simpler chants are used in each edition.

The Oxford Chant Book No. 1 (OUP). Arranged for the order of psalms as in the Revised Lectionary.

The Oxford Chant Book No. 2 (OUP). Arranged in normal numerical order and offering a selection of chants different from those of the above book.

The Oxford Chant Book for Three-Part Singing (OUP). A selection of chants arranged for S.A.B., useful for church choirs lacking tenors, or for school use.

Appendix 4. *Settings of the Holy Communion Service*

Simple congregational settings

Merbecke's setting, which was the first to be written for the English service, is to-day the most popular of congregational settings, a popularity fully justified by its musical interest and by the variety its melody obtains within the prescribed limits. It should be sung quite lightly and briskly using one of the editions (e.g. Hunt & Knight's, published by SPCK) based on Merbecke's original notation and having an accompaniment which does not continually change chords.

Martin Shaw's *An Anglican Folk Mass* (Curwen) is probably the setting most widely used after Merbecke. Optional four-part harmony is provided in the Sanctus, Benedictus and Agnus Dei. Shaw's other settings—*A Modal Setting* (Curwen) and *Parish Communion Service* (Curwen)—though conceived on lines similar to the above have not achieved the popularity of the "Folk Mass". His *Simple Setting* (Curwen) was composed on the "chantwise" principle, as was his brother Geoffrey Shaw's *Simple Modal Music* (Novello).

Gregory Murray's *People's Communion Service* might also be described as "chantwise", since it is based on one simple phrase of music which is used throughout. The setting is unison, the Creed not being included. Arthur Hutchings' *St Oswald's Music for Parish Communion* (Curwen) is another unison setting with no Creed, but is rather more challenging and of greater musical interest.

The Coventry Mass (RSCM), adapted from mediaeval sources, is a complete and simple unison setting which may be used successfully in churches where traditional music is appreciated. Rather more recognisably plainsong settings are the *Missa de Angelis,* of which the most recent edition is by Arthur Clarke (Plainchant Publications), and *Simple Traditional Music for the Eucharist*, edited by Martin Shaw (Curwen).

Modern in style

Unison settings which are modern in style include Healey Willan's *Missa de Sancta Maria Magdalena* (OUP) and L. J. White's, in E flat (OUP); the latter is without Creed. The melody line of Desmond Ratcliffe's unison *Communion Service in D* (Novello) extends over only six notes and makes no great demand on either singers or organist.

Arthur Wills' *Missa Brevis* (Novello), a recent unison setting, again without Creed is considerably more challenging and though the vocal line is not over-demanding the organ part, in which the main musical interest lies, calls for a competent player. Lloyd Webber's *Communion Service in D minor* (Novello) sustains a unison line against a fuller and more elaborate organ part; it also provides for an occasional descant or antiphonal effect between high and low voices.

Settings with a melody-line congregational range but which allow for choir altos, tenors and basses to sing their parts are useful in that they can be used as wholly unison settings if the choir is depleted, as congregational settings with the choir singing their parts or even as choir settings. Nicholson's setting in C (Faith Press) is a good example of this type, or Burton in F (RSCM. Kyrie, Sanctus, Benedictus and Agnus Dei only), while Wilson in D (Faith Press) has a tuneful appeal. Kenneth Leighton's setting for SATB choir and congregation (OUP) is more complex but equally flexible; the congregational part is duplicated by choir voice-parts but not necessarily in the treble line.

Some choir settings

Two simple and agreeable choir settings are Harris in F (RSCM. No Creed) and Hylton Stewart's *Short and Easy Setting* (OUP). Littlejohn's *Missa Sancti Niniani* (Faith Press. No Creed) and Nicholson in G (Faith Press) can also be recommended. A more ambitious choir will enjoy Sumsion in F (Novello), while for a proficient choir Darke in F (OUP) is the most effective setting of recent years.

For unaccompanied singing Charles Wood's setting in the Phrygian Mode (Faith Press) needs a competent choir, as does also the English edition of Viadana's *Missa L'Hora Passa* (Faith Press). Among less demanding settings of this kind, Batten's *Short Communion Service* (OUP), Burgess's *Missa Seraphica* (Plainchant Publications) and Waters in G (OUP. No Creed or Gloria) are worth consideration.

For choirs of boys or female choirs most of the unison settings mentioned above are suitable, and two-part choir settings for such groups include Nicholson's *Missa Choristarum* (Faith Press), Ashfield's two-part setting (Novello) and L. J. White in E major (Curwen). Martin Shaw's *Anglican Folk Mass*, other modal or plainsong settings, and the Ratcliffe setting, are well suited to men's voices, and for choir settings sung by men there is a quite simple *Missa Angelica* by Burgess (Plainchant Publications) for TBarB, and Wills' *Short Unaccompanied Service* for ATB (Novello).

APPENDIX 5. *Anthems of up to moderately easy standard*

(Some are suitable to seasons or occasions as marked)

SATB

Arcadelt, J.	*Give ear unto my prayer*	Novello	
Attwood, T.	*Teach me, O Lord*	Novello	
	Turn thy face from my sins	Novello	Lent
	Come, Holy Ghost	Novello	Whitsun
Bach, J. S.	*God liveth still*	RSCM	
	Jesu, priceless treasure	Novello, SA.279	
	Christians, shout for joy	RSCM	Easter
Bain, J.	*Brother James's Air*	OUP	
Batten, A.	**Deliver us, O Lord*	OUP	
Bevan, T.	*O Thou, who at thy Eucharist*	OUP	Communion
Blow, J.	*O pray for the peace*	Novello	
Bullock, E.	*Give laud unto the Lord*	OUP	Harvest
	Praise and salutation	OUP	Trinity
Child, W.	*Praise the Lord, O my soul*	RSCM	
Coleman, H.	*Ye servants of God*	OUP	
Cope, C.	*Give heed, my heart*	OUP	Christmas
Crotch, W.	*Comfort, O Lord*	Novello	
Drese, A.	*Round me falls the night*	SPCK	Evening
Farrant, R.	**Hide not thou thy face*	RSCM	Lent
Goss, J.	*Almighty and merciful God*	Novello	
	God so loved the world	Novello	Passiontide

Handel, G. F.	*Lord, I trust thee*	OUP	
Harris, W. H.	*Fear not, O land*	OUP	Harvest
	The Lord my pasture	Novello, SATB edn.	
Hilton, J.	**Lord, for thy tender mercy's sake*	OUP	Lent
Howells, H.	*Mine eyes for beauty pine*	OUP	
Joubert, J.	*To Mercy, Pity, Peace and Love*	Novello	
Lang, C. S.	*Good Christian men*	RSCM	Easter
Lloyd, R.	**View me, Lord*	Novello	Lent
Mendelssohn, F.	*Above all praise*	RSCM	
Mozart, W. A.	*Jesu, word of God incarnate*	Novello	Passiontide
Mudd, J. (ascr. Weelkes)	**Let thy merciful ears*	OUP	
Nicholson, S. H.	*Let us with a gladsome mind*	RSCM	Harvest
Ouseley, F. A. G.	*From the rising of the sun*	Novello	Epiphany
Palestrina, G. P. da	**O Saviour of the world*	Novello	Passiontide
Pearsall, R.	**Blessed Word of God* / *Therefore we before Him*	OUP	Communion
Pritchard, A. J.	*In heavenly love abiding*	Novello	
Purcell, H.	**Thou knowest, Lord*	Novello	
Rowley, A.	*Shepherds loud their praises*	OUP	Christmas
Schicht, arr. Ley	*The Lord ascendeth*	Novello	Ascension
Shaw, G.	*Hail, gladdening light*	Novello	
Stanford, C. V.	*O for a closer walk*	Stainer & Bell	Whitsun
Thatcher, R.	*Come, ye faithful*	OUP	Easter
Thiman, E. H.	*Sing alleluia forth*	Novello	Saints' Days

Tomblings, P.	*Sing a song of joy*	RSCM	
Tye, C.	**Hail, glorious spirits*	RSCM	Saints' Days
	**O come ye servants*	RSCM	Epiphany
Walmisley, T.	*From all that dwell*	RSCM	
Weldon, J.	*O praise God in his holiness*	Novello	
Wesley, S. S.	*Lead me, Lord*	Novello	
Whitlock, P.	*He is risen*	OUP	Easter
Williams, R. Vaughan	*O taste and see*	OUP, SATB edn.	
Wood, C.	*O most merciful*	Ascherberg	Communion

* May be sung unaccompanied, but light organ accompaniment is not objectionable.

Anthem Books: *The Oxford Easy Anthem Book* (OUP). Fifty short anthems, mainly of no great difficulty, including some two- or three-part, for various Church seasons and general use. *Church Anthem Book* (OUP), 100 anthems.

FOR OTHER COMBINATIONS OF VOICES, AND MIXED VOICES IN UNISON

Bach, J. S.	*Sing praise to God*	OUP	Unison	
Bevan, Elway	*Lord, who shall dwell*	OUP	SAB	
Carter S.	*Lord of the Dance*	Galliard	Unison	Easter
Cope, C.	*He is risen*	OUP	2-part	Easter
	Pleasure it is	OUP	SB	Harvest
Goss, J. arr. Knight, V.	*O praise the Lord*	Curwen	SAB	
Handel, G. F.	*Vouchsafe, O Lord*	Novello	SAB	
Howells, H.	*O Holy City*	Novello	Unison-and-descant	

Macpherson, C.	*Awake, my soul*	Novello	2-part	Morning
Morley, T.	*Through the day*	RSCM	SB	Evening
Rowley, A.	*Christ the Lord is risen*	Novello	Unison	Easter
	Sing to the Lord	Novello	Unison	Harvest
Sampson, G.	*O ye, who bear Christ's holy name*	Novello	Unison-and-descant	
Shaw, D.	*Now is the time of harvest-home*	Novello	Unison-and-descant	Harvest
Shaw, M.	*Hail thee, Festival Day*	Novello	SAB	Easter
	With a voice of singing	Curwen	Unison edn., also SAB edn.	
	O how manifold	Novello	Unison	Harvest
Thiman, E. H.	*We give immortal praise*	Novello	Unison-and-descant	
Tomblings, P.	*All from the sun's uprise*	OUP	SAB	
Trad. arr. Palmer	*Unto us is born a Son*	Mowbray	Unison	Christmas
Turner, C. K.	*Stand up, and bless the Lord*	OUP	SA or TB	
Wadely, F.	*At the Lamb's high feast*	OUP	Unison	Easter
Warlock, P.	*Come to Bethlehem*	Curwen	Unison edn.	Christmas
Wills, A. W.	*Sing a new song*	Novello	Unison	

Appendix 6. *Some useful guides issued by the Royal School of Church Music*

List of Recommended Church Music. Service settings and anthems for all Church seasons and occasions, showing the degree of difficulty of each piece.

"Music for Treble Voices". A list of evening service settings and anthems recommended for junior or women's choirs, showing the degree of difficulty of each piece.

List of Recommended Carols. Unison, SATB, and other combinations of voices, for Christmas, Epiphany and Easter.

Some Settings of Holy Communion (List). Suggestions for congregational settings in various styles, and simple choir settings.*

Some Church Music for Men's Voices. List of selected service settings and anthems for men's voices, with or without altos.*

Promoting Church Music. A quarterly magazine drawing attention to RSCM publications and including reviews of all new music suitable for use in parish churches.*

Easy Organ Voluntaries. A list of recommended music for the small organ.

Selected List of Recordings (English Church Choral Music). Kept up-to-date by regular supplements or new editions.

Appendix 7. *Books on elementary choir-training*

The Church Choir Trainer—H. Coleman (OUP)
Choir-Training—P. C. Saunders (RSCM)
Basic Choir-Training—E. Wright (RSCM)
Practical Choir-Training—E. C. Bairstow (RSCM)
Choirs in Little Churches—S. Morgan (Faith Press)
How to Train a Choir of Men and Women—A. J. Pritchard (RSCM)
The Training of Children's Voices—W. Carroll (Forsyth Bros.)
The Training of Boys' Voices—W. Vale (Faith Press)
Voice Production in Choral Technique (new enlarged ed.)—C. Cleall (Novello)

Appendix 8. *Organ primers and books on technique*

First Year at the Organ—P. C. Buck (Stainer & Bell)
The Organ—W. G. Alcock (Novello)
Ars Organi (complete organ method, 3 volumes)—F. Peeters (Hinrichsen)

* No charge.

The Amateur Organist—H. Coleman (OUP)
Playing the Organ—F. Routh (English Universities Press)
Modern Organ Pedalling—C. Henry Phillips (OUP)
The Elements of Extemporisation—S. H. Nicholson (RSCM)
Extemporisation for Students—R. Hunt (OUP)
Accompaniment of Plainsong—M. P. Fleming (RSCM)
Plainsong Accompaniment—J. H. Arnold (Waltham Forest)

Appendix 9. *Books of hymn tunes with varied harmonisations*

44 Hymn Tunes Freely Harmonised—E. H. Thiman (Novello)

Varied Accompaniments to 34 Well-Known Hymn Tunes—E. H. Thiman (OUP)

Varied Hymn Accompaniments—H. Coleman (OUP)

Organ Accompaniments for 24 Tunes from "English Hymnal"—E. C. Bairstow (OUP)*

Appendix 10. *Merbecke's Communion setting—recommended editions*

Merbecke, ed. Hunt & Knight (SPCK)
Merbecke, ed. Nicholson (Faith Press)
Merbecke, ed. Harwood (Novello)

The above adhere as closely as possible to Merbecke's original note-values. Other editions (e.g. Arnold's, published by OUP, and Royal Shore's published by Novello) give an equal value for each note, tending to treat the music as if it were plainsong, which it is not. The above three editions also have accompaniments which do not frequently change the chords; thus they allow for an easier flow of both words and music.

Although the Victorians can be justly credited with the revival of Merbecke's setting, their editions were misguided. Dividing the music into equal bar-lengths and adding supporting voice-parts, with constantly-changing chords, were mistakes which have resulted in a wide misinterpretation of the composer's intentions.

Appendix 11. *Organ music for manuals only*

Bach Album for Manuals Only—ed. L. Lethbridge (OUP)

Twenty Hymn-Tune Preludes for Manuals Only—C. S. Lang (OUP)

* Because of their technical difficulty these are not recommended for general use.

Twelve Short Introductory Voluntaries—W. G. Alcock (Novello)
Twenty-four Interludes on Communion Hymn Tunes—H. Coleman (OUP)
Short Organ Interludes for Liturgical Use—Dom Gregory Murray (Ascherberg) Four books.
Manual Miscellany for Organ—ed. C. H. Trevor (Elkin) 27 short pieces, all periods. Book I published in 1968.
Organ Music for Christmas, Volume II—ed. C. H. Trevor (OUP) 17 short pieces, various—16th–19th century.
"Tallis to Wesley", series—ed. G. Phillips (Hinrichsen) Volumes 1, 5, 18, 21, 22 and 24. The series comprises some 36 volumes, most of which contain two-stave music.
Old English Organ Music for Manuals—ed. C. H. Trevor (OUP) Four books, about 18 short pieces in each.
Three Voluntaries by Greene, Boyce and Stanley—ed. Campbell (OUP)
Two-stave Voluntaries by Modern Composers (Novello) Two books with ten pieces in each.
For Manuals Only (OUP) Eight pieces, old and new.
Hymn-Tune Preludes—R. Groves (Elkin) Books I and II (general), Book III (plainsong), Book IV (Welsh).
Seasonal Chorale Preludes for Manuals Only—ed. C. H. Trevor (OUP) 53 pieces from 17th–18th centuries. Book I (Advent to Passiontide), Book II (Easter, Whitsun, Trinity, General).
Two short pieces in F (Air and Gavotte)—Samuel Wesley ed. Basil Ramsey (Novello)
Twenty-four Pieces—J. Langlais (UMP) Two books.
Les Maîtres Français de l'Orgue—ed. F. Raugel (UMP) Two volumes, 16th–17th century composers.
Au Pied de l'Autel—J. Guy Ropartz (UMP) Two volumes.
Twenty-four Pieces in Free Style—L. Vierne (UMP) Two books.
Thirty-five Miniatures—F. Peeters (Hinrichsen) Volumes I and II.
Old Masters (Universal Edition). Six volumes 13 to 21 pieces in each, composers such as Sweelinck, Buxtehude, Pachelbel, Krebs, Mozart).
Twelve Easy Chorale Preludes—Telemann (Hinrichsen)
Twelve Short Keyboard Works—Pachelbel (Hinrichsen)
Piccola Antologia—ed. Ravanello (Hinrichsen) Twelve pieces by old Italian composers.
Fiori dell'Organo (Universal Edition) Volume I (Eighteen pieces,

Sweelinck to J. S. Bach), Volume II (Eighteen pieces, J. S. Bach to César Franck).

APPENDIX 12. *Organ Voluntaries of easy to moderate difficulty*

An Introduction to Bach—ed. A. Henderson (Bayley & Ferguson)

The Organist's Bach—ed. O. A. Mansfield (Paxton) Inexpensive collection of twenty short pieces.

Nine Easy Pieces by J. S. Bach—ed. Coates (Ashdown)

Eight Short Preludes & Fugues—J. S. Bach (Novello)

A First Organ Album—ed. L. Lethbridge (OUP) Six pieces, 17th–18th century.

The Progressive Organist—ed. C. H. Trevor (Elkin) A series of albums of about eighteen pieces each, 17th–19th century, Volume I to Grade IV Associated Board Standard, Volume II to Grade V standard, Volume III to Grade VI, etc.

Seasonal Choral Preludes (with Pedals)—ed. C. H. Trevor (OUP) Book I (Advent to Passiontide), Book II (Easter, Whitsun, General).

Second Book of Wedding Pieces—ed. C. H. Trevor (OUP) Fifteen short pieces, mainly 17th–18th century, useful for festival occasions.

Organ Book No. 1—ed. C. H. Trevor (OUP) 16 pieces, 16th to 19th century.

Funeral Music—Tallis, ed. M. and G. Shaw (Curwen)

Suite for Organ—J. Stanley, ed. Coleman (OUP)

Album of Trumpet Tunes—Purcell (Ashdown)

Four Pieces from "Abdelazar"—Purcell arr. Ratcliffe (Novello)

Three Pieces from "Music for the Royal Fireworks"—Handel, ed. Blake (OUP)

"Water Music" Suite—Handel, arr. O. Peasgood (Novello)

A Handel Organ Album—ed. S. de B. Taylor (OUP) Thirteen arrangements.

Vountary in C minor—M. Greene (Novello)

A Little Tune—W. Felton (Cramer)

Selected Slow Movements from "Six Organ Sonatas"—Mendelssohn, ed. P. J. Mansfield (OUP)

Ten Hymn-Tune Voluntaries—H. Coleman (Stainer & Bell) Two books, five pieces in each.

Five Short and Easy Pieces—C. Hylton Stewart (Novello) Based on hymn-tunes.

Five Fancies for Small Organ—N. Ponsonby (Novello)

Three Short and Easy Postludes—F. Wadely (Novello)

Six Short Preludes and Postludes—C. V. Stanford (Stainer & Bell)

A Little Organ Book (Ascherberg) Short pieces written in memory of Sir Hubert Parry.

Elegy—Parry (Novello)

Book of Simple Organ Voluntaries (OUP) Six pieces by Sumsion, Darke, Murrill, etc.

Preludes and Voluntaries—E. Thiman (Curwen) Three books.

"Folk Tune", "Scherzo" and "Andante Tranquillo" (from "Five Pieces")—Whitlock (OUP)

An Easy Album (OUP) Six pieces by modern English composers.

Six Organ Preludes on Chorales—D. Buxtehude, ed. Ley (OUP) For Advent to Whitsun.

Toccata in F—J. L. Krebs (Cramer)

Liber Organi (Schott) Volume I (pieces by early French masters), Volume III (early Spanish), Volume IV (early Italian), Volume VI (early German), Volume X (old English).

Church Organist's Golden Treasury—ed. Pfatteicher and Davison (Universal Edition). Three volumes of altogether 200 choral preludes of the classical period.

Quiet Movements from Rheinberger—ed. Lloyd Webber (Ascherberg)

Suite Gothique—L. Boellmann (Ashdown)

Eleven Choral Preludes—Brahms (Novello)

Seven Chorale Improvisations—S. Karg-Elert (Paxton)

Marche Triomphale "Nun Danket"—S. Karg-Elert (Breitkopf)

Aria—F. Peeters (Hinrichsen)

APPENDIX 13. *Books with special reference to organ accompaniment of services*

The Beginning Organist—E. H. Thiman (Ascherberg)

Playing a Church Organ—M. P. Conway (Marshall, Morgan & Scott)

The ABC of Church Music—S. Rhys and K. Palmer (Hodder & Stoughton) Several relevant chapters.

(See also Appendix 8)

APPENDIX 14. *Principles of the Royal School of Church Music*

1. In church music, it is essential, even more than in secular music,

to maintain the highest possible standard, particularly in the fundamental principles of:

Singing correct notes
Singing in tune
Quality of tone
Attack and unanimity
Blend and balance of voices
Absolute clarity of words

2. The words in responses, psalms and canticles should be said or sung with proper emphasis and without distortion.

3. The proper rendering of the simple parts of services is of first importance.

4. Choirs are the responsible leaders of the congregation whether in the sung or spoken parts of the service.

5. Choirs have a duty to set an example of reverence and devotion in church.

APPENDIX 15. *Facilities offered by the Royal School of Chuch Music*

Advice on all matters concerning church music, choirs, organs. Personal visits by Special Commissioners to choirs in their own churches. Courses ranging from a half-day to a week, at headquarters and local centres, for juniors or adults concerned in various ways with the ordering of music in worship. Festival services locally or regionally arranged. Quarterly magazines. Publications, musical or instructional, at low cost to members, and facilities for obtaining music and books of any publisher. Choir badges and useful equipment for the church choir. Special "Chorister Training Scheme" for recruiting and encouragement of junior singers.

APPENDIX 16. *Handbooks on conducting*

Conducting for Church Musicians—H. Coleman (RSCM)
Handbook on the Technique of Conducting—Sir Adrian Boult (Paterson)

APPENDIX 17. *Modern hymn tunes in a generally "traditional" vein*

This list is by no means exhaustive but is representative of some worthwhile examples of the type of tune in question.

Ancient and Modern Revised (1950 edition) provides by far the widest choice of tunes in this category:

237. *Amen Court* (Dykes Bower).
407 (ii). *Standish* (Dykes Bower).
155. *Naphill* (Darke).
297. *Ladywell* (W. H. Ferguson). } Both first-rate examples.
331. *Wolvercote* (W. H. Ferguson). }
306. *Crucis victoria* (Foster).
235. *North Petherton* (W. H. Harris).
298 (i). *Alberta* (W. H. Harris).
528 (i). *Sennen Cove* (W. H. Harris).
256. *Thornbury* (Harwood). } Two more highly commendable tunes.
375. *Luckington* (Harwood). }
417. *Sheen* (Holst).
579. *Thaxted* (Holst).
102. *Love Unknown* (Ireland).
369. *Northampton* (King).
215. *Bow Brickhill* (Nicholson).
302. *Totteridge* (Nicholson).
453. *Airlie* (Nicholson).
182. *Marching* (Martin Shaw).
269. *Little Cornard* (Martin Shaw).
224 (i). *Corona* (Hylton Stewart).
257 (i). *Abbot's Leigh* (C. V. Taylor).

The English Hymnal offers much less in this particular field:

141. *Gonfalon Royal* (Percy Buck).
633. *Mont Richard* (Percy Buck).
419. *St. Botolph* (Gordon Slater).
454. *Temple* (Walford Davies).
152. *Down Ampney* (Vaughan Williams).
641. *Sine Nomine* (Vaughan Williams).

RSCM publications include a number of tunes mentioned above. In addition, the following are recommended:

From Festival Service Book No. 1: *Dutch National Anthem* (arranged by Martin How) to the words "Thy Kingdom come, O God".
From Music for Evensong (Set D): *Lauderdale* (Leonard Blake) to the words "O God, before whose altar" (A. and M. Revised 340).

APPENDIX 18.

SIMPLICITY IN A MODERN IDIOM

by ALAN GIBBS

There is a need for church music which is lively and modern, yet not too difficult for the average church choir. Three works which may be said to point the way to the achievement of this double standard are:

Alexander Goehr: *Virtutes* (Schott), particularly
No. 1—Verse (Whatsoever things are true)
No. 2b—The Man of Life
No. 5—O Gracious God

Alan Ridout: *Magnificat and Nunc Dimittis in E,* for trebles (Stainer)

Martin Dalby: *A Shorter Benedicite* (Ascherberg)

In Goehr we find avoidance of extremes of compass: the tenor part rarely touches E, for instance. Intervals are used vocally by all three composers. This does not mean so much that they exclude unfamiliar ones (although they do), as that they treat leaps naturally, as in plainsong and Palestrina, by returning within the leap. Maxwell Davies, in the four carols from *"O Magnum Mysterium"* (Schott) seeks simplicity by another method—a freer use of chromatic intervals, but restriction of each vocal part to a few different notes (a technique taken even further in Jonathan Harvey's *Carol* (Novello)): however, apart from *"Fader of Heven"*, these had best be reserved for young, enterprising singers under the directorship of a musician with a first-class ear. Ridout is almost completely diatonic, the *Magnificat* using only the notes of the E major scale, and the *Nunc dimittis* the notes of E (Aeolian) minor with one odd F natural. Dalby's method is a good application of folk technique—diatonic in the keys through which it passes except for the sharpening or flattening of notes according to their context (compare the tunings of the seventh in the best-known version of *"A Virgin most pure"*). All three composers respect the atavistic appeal of modal melody, which turns up nowadays alike in the compositions of young children, pop songs ("Eleanor Rigby" for instance), Gelineau and the best modern hymn-tunes, such as John Gardner's *St. Olaf's* in the Cambridge Hymnal.

Textures involving four or more real parts require the maximum effort and rehearsal time. Composers are wise to seek methods of scoring and techniques which make learning and rehearsal easier when they have the average church or school choir in mind. Goehr's *Verse* is in unison (octaves)—the easiest solution if compass permits—with one two-note chord at the end. Dalby's piece permits of an alternative unison rendering. In the Cambridge Hymnal there is a host of fine unison pieces in a genuine modern vein, while the following also deserve consideration:

Desmond Ratcliffe: *A Communion Trilogy* (Novello)
Alan Ridout: *Mass of St. Peter* (Stainer)

Goehr's No. 2b varies its textures: verses 1 and 4 are in unison; 2 and 5 are a two-part canon, SA against TB; and 3 and 6 have S doubling T and A doubling B, first in the same rhythm, then in canon, finally in unison. ST–AB doubling is overdone by many composers in ambitious works, where it should be reserved for climaxes or special effects, but its use (in moderation) has every justification in pieces aiming at simplicity of performance.

Matyas Seiber: *Missa Brevis* (in Latin) (Curwen)

is at the same time an expressive liturgical piece and a study in two parts which makes use of this scoring technique, as well as canon and invertible counterpoint. Parts of it, besides the *Kyrie,* could be used effectively as motets in Anglican worship. In Goehr's No. 5, the tenors and basses share a part—a godsend for choirs with weakness in these departments or girls chary of singing tenor (see Charles Cleall's *Voice Production in Choral Technique,* Novello)! A fine SAB piece, with the bass dividing at the end, is:

Zoltan Kodaly: *Veni Emmanuel* (in Latin or English) (Boosey)

Other scorings which modern church composers might experiment with include doublings at two octaves distance and a true choral unison. We can learn much from the French and Hungarians that will make our choral music more colourful.

There are some good unaccompanied modern pieces in four real parts which are not too long or difficult:

Stravinsky: *Ave Maria* (in Latin) (Boosey)
Stravinsky: *Pater Noster* (in Latin)) (Boosey)
Richard Rodney Bennett: *Three Verses* (Universal) Nos. 1 and 2
Britten: *The Holly and the Ivy* (Boosey)

The last piece has a fourth verse that is not easy for the Sopranos and Altos, but the traditional theme holds the whole piece together. It is also printed in the Cambridge Hymnal, where there are a number of beautiful commissioned items well worth performing by choirs, for instance Berkeley's gem *"I sing of a maiden"*, and Wordsworth's *"Ah my dear Lord"*. A little more difficult, but good for teaching the choir self-assurance in entries at the interval of a second, is:

Gordon Hawkins: *As the hart panteth* (Oxford)

An invigorating carol of the same standard of difficulty is:

Alan Ridout: *Hymn of the Nativity* (Stainer)

And another, more expressive and requiring a larger choir (there is a semi-chorus) is:

Britten: *Hymn to the Virgin* (Boosey)

These are all unaccompanied, and any choirmaster hoping to have a choir capable of singing modern music (or *anything* unaccompanied) had better begin by practising unison and two-part exercises with an ear to intonation. Kodaly's *"Let us sing correctly"*, his *Bicinia Hungarica* and other books (Boosey) form a thorough-going method of this sort, and smaller pieces in two parts include the Seiber Mass above and:

Maxwell Davies: *Fader of Heven* (Schott)

A worthwhile setting of the mass in four parts, with organ, from which at least one movement might be prepared for a special occasion, is:

Berkeley: *Missa Brevis*, available in English (Chester)

The organ's rôle needs to be considered. In the Ridout and Dalby canticles we have the models: chords simple (two- and three-part) except at climaxes—how many organist-composers forget what is obvious to non-organists who come to write for the instrument, that sonorous writing does not mean fistfuls of notes but well-placed ones, with appropriate use of 4′ and 16′ (etc.) registration! Their provision of frequent rests is helpful for the organist-conductor. And they both save pedal entries for points of climax. When the pedal does enter, it is mainly slow-moving. Both works can be performed on an instrument without pedals if need be. The organist's relationship with the choir is also considered—leads are given surreptitiously in the course of a seemingly independent part discussing other material. Rhythmic support is provided by the organ in the form of strong beats against which the choir may project syncopations (a technique also used in Kenneth Leighton's congregational *Te Deum* for Monkton Combe (Novello)). Goehr's *Verse* follows another model: an Orff-like figure is repeated in an ostinato manner. Another idea that might be taken up is in Goehr's No. 5: the organ plays only a pedal anchorage against which the voices measure their intonation, and the organist's arms are free to conduct! Instrumental doubling of voice parts in "unaccompanied" items is allowable *if* the character of the piece calls for it and *if* it is done tastefully. The BBC has supported Bruckner and Nono in this fashion, and it is better for a church choir to attempt Stravinsky's *Ave Maria* with the organ playing weak, or missing, parts than not at all.

The principle of repetition, observable in the simplest folk song, is another gift to composers who wish to write simple music. Ternary form is the obvious setting for a number of liturgical texts: Britten accepts the gambit in the *Kyrie* of the *Missa Brevis*, and we notice this even if we do not notice that the *Christe* is an inversion of the *Kyrie*. The infinite variety in the use of repetition and variation in plainsong is an object lesson for any intending church composer—see the three phrases of *Missa de Angelis*, or the near-sonata-form of the Mass IV Gloria on which Merbecke based his own. Dalby's canticle expands, contracts and varies one theme throughout; Ridout's *Magnificat* repeats most of its opening material, and the *Nunc dimittis* is a minor variation on it. It is surprising that the verse anthem has not produced more modern imitations: many choirs have a soloist who could cope with verse sections while the rest need only learn the refrain (this could be the same each time, with different accompaniments).

Since children are more amenable to modern idioms than their elders, it is worth mentioning a few treble pieces whose difficulties are not inordinate:

- Colin Mawby: *Four Psalm Settings* (Ascherberg). These are in two parts, and have alternative lower notes to produce an F sharp ceiling.
- Ridout: *Sacred Songs* (three sets, Stainer). Unison. Some are simpler than others, and just as rewarding (e.g. *Come, my way*" in the first set)
- John Davey: *O praise God in his holiness* (Ascherberg). Slight, but jolly, in two parts.
- Francis Jackson: *Evening Canticles for trebles* (RSCM).
- Richard Rodney Bennett: *Two Lullabies* (Universal). These are more difficult, being for unaccompanied SSA, but are very sweet.

And again I say . . . don't forget the Cambridge Hymnal!